# MOHAM

AND

# MOHAMMEDANISM:

## LECTURES

DELIVERED AT THE

ROYAL INSTITUTION OF GREAT BRITAIN

IN FEBRUARY AND MARCH, 1874.

By R. BOSWORTH SMITH, M.A.,

ASSISTANT MASTER IN HARROW SCHOOL, LATE FELLOW OF TRINITY COLLEGE, OXFORD.

## THE BOOK TREE
SAN DIEGO, CALIFORNIA

Originally published 1875
Harper & Brothers Publishers
New York

New material, revisions and cover
©2002
The Book Tree
All rights reserved

ISBN 1-58509-085-9

Cover layout and design
Lee Berube

Printed on Acid-Free Paper
in the United States and United Kingdom
by LightningSource, Inc.

Published by
**The Book Tree**
P O Box 16476
San Diego, CA 92176

We provide fascinating and educational products to help awaken the public to new ideas and
information that would not be available otherwise.
Call 1 (800) 700-8733 for our *FREE BOOK TREE CATALOG*

# FOREWARD

In today's world Western culture is making an effort to understand the religion of Islam (Mohammedanism) because we have been forced to confront it in ways that we would have never imagined in the past. Islam has been the fastest growing religion in the world for many decades, and was founded by the prophet Mohammed, who lived from approximately C.E. 570-632.

The vast majority of Muslims are peace-loving people who have no interest in taking part in hatred, violence or murder. This book does not preach such hatred—on the contrary, the author wanted it to serve as a bridge between the Islamic and Christian worlds. There is room for understanding and compassion between these worlds and the author brings forth strong similarities between these belief structures as a foundation for growth and mutual respect.

Some scholars have put forth the idea that Islam and Christianity are on a "collision course", with no chance for harmony due to immense differences in culture. This book proclaims the exact opposite—that the common threads between these worlds are so strong that we can afford to appreciate our cultural differences. The richness of our diversity can be celebrated rather than fought over, due to amazing resemblances in the belief systems as outlined in this book.

Smith states that Jesus and Mohammed, due to their contributions to the world, belong next to each other on the scale of things, as opposed to one (no matter which one) being above the other. If such recognition could occur, on equal terms from both religions, then a mutual respect between them would result. Long out of print, this book has the potential to contribute important ideas of harmony and respect between faiths.

Paul Tice

# UXORI MEÆ,

NULLIUS NON LABORIS PARTICIPI,

HUJUSCE PRÆSERTIM OPUSCULI INSTIGATRICI ET ADMINISTRÆ,

STUDIORUM COMMUNITATIS

HAS, QUALESCUNQUE SINT, PRIMITIAS

DEDICO.

# PREFACE.

THE substance of these Lectures was written early in 1872 : they were originally intended only for a select audience of friends at Harrow, but on the suggestion of some of those who heard them they were afterward considerably enlarged, and were delivered before the Royal Institution of Great Britain in the months of February and March, 1874.

They are an attempt, however imperfect, within a narrow compass, but, it is hoped, from a somewhat comprehensive and independent point of view, to render justice to what was great in Mohammed's character, and to what has been good in Mohammed's influence on the world. To original Oriental research they lay no claim, nor indeed to much originality at all—perhaps the subject hardly now admits of it; but, thanks to the numerous translations of the Koran into European languages, and to the great works of Oriental scholars, such as Caussin de Perceval, Sprenger, Muir, and Deutsch, the materials for forming an impartial judgment of the Prophet of Arabia are within the reach of any earnest student of the Science of Religion, and of all who care, as those who have ever studied Mohammed's character must care, for the deeper problems of the human soul.

The value of the estimate formed of the influence of Mohammedanism on the world at large must, of course, depend upon such a modicum of general historical knowledge, and such catholic sympathies, as the writer has been able, amid other pressing duties, to bring to his work. The only qualification he would venture to claim for himself in the matter is that of a sympathetic interest in his subject, and of a conscientious desire first to divest himself of all preconceived ideas, and then by a careful study of the Koran itself, and afterward of its best expounders, to arrive as nearly as may be at the truth. How vast is the interval between his wishes and his performance the author knows full well, and any one who has ever been fairly fascinated with a great subject will know also; for he will have felt that to have the will is not always to have the power, and that the framing of an ideal implies the consciousness of failure to attain to it.

A Christian who retains that paramount allegiance to Christianity which is his birthright, and yet attempts, without favor and without prejudice, to portray another religion, is inevitably exposed to misconstruction. In the study of his subject he will have been struck sometimes by the extraordinary resemblance between his own creed and another, sometimes by the sharpness of the contrast; and, in order to avoid those misrepresentations, which are, unfortunately, never so common as where they ought to be unknown—in the discussion of religious questions—he will be tempted, in filling in the portrait, to project his own personal predilections on the canvas, and to bring the differences into full relief, while he leaves the resemblances in shadow. And yet a comparison between two

systems, if it is to have any fruitful results, if
its object is to unite rather than divide, if, in
short, it is to be of the spirit of the Founder of
Christianity, must, in matters of religion above
all, be based on what is common to both.   There
is, in the human race, in spite of their manifold
diversities, a good deal of human nature; enough,
at all events, to entitle us to assume that the
Founders of any two religious systems which
have had a great and continued hold upon a
large part of mankind must have had many
points of contact.  Accordingly, in comparing,
as he has done to some extent, the founder of
Islam with the Founder of Christianity—a comparison which, if it were not expressed, would
always be implied — the author of these Lectures has thought it right mainly to dwell on
that aspect of the character of Christ, which,
being admitted by Mussulmans as well as Christians, by foes as well as friends, may possibly
serve as a basis, if not for an ultimate agreement,
at all events for an agreement to differ from
one another upon terms of greater sympathy
and forbearance, of understanding and of respect.

That Islam will ever give way to Christianity in the East, however much we may desire it, and whatever good would result to the world, it is difficult to believe; but it is certain that Mohammedans may learn much from Christians and yet remain Mohammedans, and that Christians have something at least to learn from Mohammedans, which will make them not less but more Christian than they were before. If we would conquer Nature, we must first obey her; and the Fourth Lecture is an attempt to show, from a full recognition of the facts of Nature underlying both religions — of the points of difference as well as of resemblance —that Mohammedanism, if it can never become actually one with Christianity, may yet, by a process of mutual approximation and mutual understanding, prove its best ally. In other words, the author believes that their is a unity above and beyond that unity of Christendom which, properly understood, all earnest Christians so much desire: a unity which rests upon the belief that " the children of one Father may worship him under different names;" that they may be influenced by one spirit, even though they know it not; that they may all have one hope, even if they have not one faith.

HARROW, *April* 15, 1873.

---

I have to return my best thanks to my friend Mr. AR-THUR WATSON, for a careful revision of my manuscript, and for several valuable suggestions.

It may be serviceable to English readers to mention the more accessible works upon the subject, to the writers of which I desire here to express my general obligations, over and above the acknowledgment, in the text, wherever I am conscious of them, of special debts. I am the more anxious to do this fully here, as, while I am quite aware that I could not have written on this subject at all without making their labors the basis of mine, I have yet in the exercise of my own judgment often been obliged to criticise their reasonings and their conclusions. I can only hope that even where I have ventured to express a somewhat vehement dissent from my authorities, they will kindly credit me with something at least of the *verecunde dissentio* which becomes a learner, and of the zeal for truth, or for his idea of it, which becomes a writer, however diffident of himself, on a great subject.

"The Koran," translated by Sale, with an elaborate Introduction and full Notes drawn from the Arabic Commentators (1734).

"The Koran," translated by Savary (1782), also with instructive explanatory Notes.

"The Koran," translated by Rodwell (1861): the Suras arranged, as far as possible, chronologically.

----

Gagnier's "Vie de Mahomet" (1732); drawn chiefly from Abul Feda and the Sonna.

Gibbon's "Decline and Fall of the Roman Empire;" Chapters L., LI., LII. (1788). A most masterly and complete picture.

Weil's "Mohamed der Prophet" (1845). Able and to the point.

Caussin de Perceval's "Essai sur l'Histoire des Arabes," etc. (1847), gives particularly full information upon the obscure subject of early Arabian history, and is written from an absolutely neutral point of view.

Sprenger's "Life of Mohammad," Allahabad, 1851; and his greater work, 'Das Leben und die Lehre des Mohamad' (1851–1861), the most exhaustive, original, and learned of all, but by no means the most impartial: he is often, as I shall point out on one or two occasions in the notes, flagrantly unfair to Mohammed.

Sir William Muir's "Life of Mahomet" (1858–1861). Learned and comprehensive, able and fair; though its scientific value is somewhat impaired by theological assumptions as to the nature of inspiration, and by the introduction of a personal Ahriman, which, while it is self-contradictory in its supposed operation, seems to me only to create new difficulties, instead of solving old ones.

"The Talmud," an article in the *Quarterly Review* (October, 1867); "Islam," an article in the *Quarterly Review* (October, 1869): both full of most recondite Eastern learning. Had the lamented author lived to finish the work he shadowed forth in the last of these, he would probably have drawn a juster and more vivid picture of Islam as a whole than has ever yet been given to the world.

--------

For less elaborate works :

Ockley's " History of the Saracens from 632–705." Picturesque ; dealing largely in romance (1708–1718).

Hallam's " Middle Ages," Chapter VI. (1818) ; Milman's " Latin Christianity," Book IV., Chapters I. and II. (1857) ; both good samples of the high merits of each as an historian.

Carlyle's " Hero as Prophet " (1846). Most stimulating.

Washington Irving's " Life of Mahomet " (1849). The work of a novelist, but strangely divested of all romance.

Lecture by Dean Stanley in his " Eastern Church " (1862). Has the peculiar charm of all the author's writings. Catholic in its sympathies, and suggestive, as well from his treatment of the subject as from the place the author assigns to it on the borders of, if not within, the Eastern Church itself.

Barthélemy St. Hilaire's " Mahomet et le Koran " (1865), a comprehensive and very useful review of most of what has been written on the subject.

--------

On the general subject of Comparative Religion :

" Religions of the World," by F. D. Maurice (1846). Perhaps of all his writings the one which best shows us the character and mind of the man.

" Études d'Histoire Religieuse," by Renan (1858). Ingenious and fascinating, but not always, nor indeed often, convincing.

" Les Religions et les Philosophies dans l'Asie Centrale," by Gobineau (1866), gives the best account extant of Bâbyism in Persia.

" Chips from a German Workshop " (1868), and " Introduction to the Science of Religion " (1873), by Max Müller. Unfortunately the author says very little about Mohammedanism, but from him I have derived some very valuable suggestions as to the general treatment of the subject. Perhaps it is well that the extraordinary learning and genius of Mr. Max Müller should be given mainly to subjects which are less within the reach of ordinary European students than is Islam, but it is impossible not to wish that he may some day give the world a " Chip " or two on the Religion of Mohammed.

---

For books which throw light on the specialties of Mohammedanism in different countries:

Al-Makkari's " History of the Mohammedan Dynasties in Spain " (Eng. Trans.).

Sir John Malcolm's " History of Persia " (1815).

Condé's " History of the Dominion of the Arabs in Spain " (1820–21).

Crawfurd's " Indian Archipelago " (1820).

Colonel Briggs's " Rise of the Mohammedan Power in India," translated from the Persian of Ferishta (1829).

Sir Stamford Raffles's " History of Java " (2d edition), (1830).

Burckhardt's " Travels in Arabia " (1829).

Caillé's " Travels through Central Africa to Timbuctoo " (1830).

Burckhardt's " Notes on the Bedouins and Wah-Habees " (1831).

Lane's " Modern Egyptians " (1836).

Burton's " Pilgrimage to Mecca and Medina " (1856).

Barth's " Travels in Central Africa " (1857).

Waitz's " Anthropologie der Naturvölker " (Leipsig, 1860).

Lane's " Notes to his Translation of the Thousand and One Nights " (new edition, edited by E. S. Poole, 1865).

Elphinstone's " History of India " (3d edition), (1866).

Palgrave's " Arabia " (1867).

" Our Indian Mussulmans," by W. W. Hunter (1871).

Burton's "Zanzibar" (1872).

Shaw's "High Tartary, Yarkand, and Kashgar" (1871).

Palgrave's "Essays on Eastern Subjects" (1872).

"Report of the General Missionary Conference at Allahabad" (1873).

Three articles in periodical literature, besides "Islam" mentioned above, are of very high merit, and have furnished me, in enlarging my work, with some matter for reflection or criticism:

"Mahomet," *National Review* (July, 1858).

"The Great Arabian," *National Review* (October, 1861).

"Mahomet," *British Quarterly Review* (January, 1872).

------

Among other works which I regret I have not been able to consult may be mentioned:

Gerock's "Versuch einer Darstellung der Christologie des Koran" (Homburg, 1839).

Freeman's "Lectures on the History and Conquests of the Saracens" (1856).

Geiger's "Was hat Mohammed aus dem Judenthume aufgenommen?"

Nöldeke's "Geschichte des Qorans."

"Essays on the Life of Mohammed and subjects subsidiary thereto," by Syed Ahmed Khan Bahador (1870).

"A Critical Examination of the Life and Teachings of Mohammed," by Syed Ameer Ali Moulla (1873).

The last two books I had not heard of when I wrote the substance of these Lectures; and in enlarging my work, I have purposely abstained from consulting them, as I have been given to understand that from a Mohammedan point of view they advocate something of the spirit and arrive at some of the results which it had been my object to urge from the Christian stand-point. I would not, of course, venture to compare my own imperfect work, derived as it is in the main from the study of books in the European languages, and from reflection upon the materials they supply, with works drawn, as I presume, directly from the fountain-head. But if the starting-points be different, and the routes entirely independent of each other, and yet there turns out to be a similarity in the results arrived at, possibly each may feel greater confidence that there is something of value in his conclusions.

# CONTENTS.

## LECTURE I.

### INTRODUCTORY.

## LECTURE II.

### MOHAMMED.

# *LECTURE III.*

## Mohammedanism.

# *LECTURE IV.*

## Mohammedanism and Christianity.

# LECTURES

DELIVERED AT THE

ROYAL INSTITUTION OF GREAT BRITAIN

IN FEBRUARY AND MARCH, 1874.

# LECTURE I.

DELIVERED AT THE ROYAL INSTITUTION, LONDON,
FEBRUARY 14, 1874.

## INTRODUCTORY.

Sua cuique genti religio est, nostra nobis.—CICERO.

'Αλλ' ἐν παντὶ ἔθνει ὁ φοβούμενος αὐτὸν, καὶ ἐργαζόμενος δικαιοσύνην, δεκτὸς αὐτῷ ἐστι.—ST. PETER.

THE Science of Comparative Religion is still in its infancy; and if there is one danger more than another against which it should be on its guard, it is that of hasty and ill-considered generalization. Hasty generalization is the besetting temptation of all young Sciences; may I not say of Science in general? They are in too great a hurry to justify their existence by arriving at results which may be generally intelligible, instead of waiting patiently till the result shapes itself from the premises; as if, in the pursuit of truth, the chase was not always worth more than the game, and the process itself more than the result. Theory has, it is true, its advant-

ages, even in a young Science, in the way of suggesting
a definite line which inquiry may take. A brilliant hypothesis formed, not by random guess-work, but by the
trained imagination of the man of Science, or by the
true divination of genius, enlarges the horizon of the
student whom the limits of the human faculties themselves drive to be a specialist, but who is apt to become
too much so. It throws a flood of light upon a field of
knowledge which was before, perhaps, half in shadow,
bringing out each object in its relative place and in its
true proportions; finally, it gathers scattered facts into
one focus, and, explaining them provisionally by a single
law, it makes an appeal to the fancy, which must react
on the other mental powers, and be a most powerful
stimulus to further research. In truth, much that is now
demonstrated fact was once hypothesis, and would never
have been demonstrated unless it had been first assumed.
But since there are few Keplers in the world — men
ready to sacrifice, without hesitation, an hypothesis that
had seemed to explain the universe, and become, as it
were, a part of themselves, the moment that the facts
seem to require it—great circumspection will always be
needed lest the facts may be made to bend to the theory,
instead of its being modified to meet them.

Bearing this caution in mind, we may, perhaps, think
that the Science of Comparative Religion, young as it

is, has yet been in existence long enough to enable us to lay it down, at all events provisionally, as a general law, that all the great religions of the world, the commencement of which has not been immemorial—coeval, that is, with the human mind itself—have been in the first instance moral rather than theological; they have been called into existence to meet social and national needs; they have raised man gradually toward God, rather than brought down God at once to man.

Judaism, for instance, sprang into existence at the moment when the Israelites passed, and because they passed, from the Patriarchal to the Political life; when from slavery they emerged into freedom; when they ceased to be a family, and became a nation. " I am the Lord thy God, which brought thee out of the land of Egypt, and out of the house of bondage." The Moral Law which followed—the Theocracy itself—was the outcome of this fundamental fact. The nation that God has chosen—nay, that he has called into existence—is to keep his laws and to be his people. Consequently, all law to the ancient Hebrew was alike divine, whether written, as he believed, by the finger of God on two tables, or whether applied by the civil magistrate to the special cases brought before him. Moral and political offenses are thus offenses against God, and the ideas of crime and sin are identical alike in fact and in thought.

Again, take a glance at the religion of Buddha. We
speak of Buddhism, and are apt to think of it chiefly as
a body of doctrine, drawn up over two thousand years
ago, and at this day professed by four hundred and fifty
millions of human beings; and we wonder, as well we
may, how a *summum bonum* of mere painlessness in
this world, and practically, and to the ordinary mind, of
total extinction when this world is over, can have satisfied the spiritual cravings of Buddha's contemporaries,
and in its various forms can now be the life-guidance
of a third of the human race. But we forget that, in its
origin at least, Buddhism was more of a social than of a
religious reformation. It was an attack upon that web
of priestcraft which Brahmanism had woven around the
whole frame-work of Indian society.* It was the level-
ing of caste distinctions, the sight of a " man born to be
a king " throwing off his royal dignity, sweeping away
the sacerdotal mummeries which he had himself tested
and found unfruitful, preferring poverty to riches, and
Sûdras to Brahmans. It was Buddha's overpowering
sense of the miseries of sin, his dim yearnings after a
better life, his moral system—of which the sum is Love

---

* See Max Müller's " Chips from a German Workshop," vol. i., p. 210
-226, especially p. 220; and Spence Hardy's " Legends and Theories
of the Buddhists," Introduction, p. 13-20. Cf. also Beal's " Buddhist
Pilgrims," Introduction, p. 49, seq.

—which wrought upon the hearts of his hearers. "He founded, it is true, a new religion, but he began by attacking an old." He reconstructed society first, and it was his social reform that led to his religion, rather than his religion which involved his social reconstruction. The half we may, perhaps, think would have been more than the whole—

"Quæsivit cœlo lucem ingemuitque repertâ."

Nor is it much otherwise with Christianity itself. Christ was before all things the Founder of a new Society; not, it is true, of a political Society: had it been so, more of his countrymen would have seen in his person the Messiah that was to come, and in his kingdom the golden age of their own poets and prophets. The political frame-work, indeed, of the world Christ came neither to destroy nor to reconstruct, except indirectly and remotely. He recognized the logic of facts; above all, the tremendous logic of the Roman Empire. Tribute was to be paid to Cæsar, even though that Cæsar was a Tiberius. The new Society was potentially a world-wide one, a vast democracy in which Jew and Roman, slave and freeman, rich and poor were on a footing of absolute equality. Enthusiastic love to Christ himself, evidenced by purity of heart, by forgetfulness of self, and by enthusiastic love to all mankind, was the one condition and the one test of membership.

It is true that to this new Creation of his Christ gives a name, which we are accustomed to look upon as conveying mainly theological ideas; he calls it " the Kingdom of Heaven," but how does he explain the term himself? His great precursor, John the Baptist, had predicted its immediate advent. Christ says, It is here already—it is *within* you. At the very opening of his work, he speaks of it as already existing; the outline was there, even if the details were not filled in. Now if the Kingdom of Heaven existed before it had dawned, even upon the most favored of his followers, that he was more than " that Prophet," it would seem to follow that the essence of his kingdom was, not the doctrine which they did not and could not as yet accept, but the higher life they saw Christ leading—the life of the soul; and which, seeing, they reverenced, and reverencing, as far as might be, wished to imitate. The Sermon on the Mount, so far as that which is indescribable can be described at all, and that which is the fountain-head of goodness in infinitely varied types can be judged by one or two of the rills which issue from it, is little else than Christ's own life translated into words; and those who, least imperfectly, retranslated his words back into their own lives, were the very " salt of the earth." They were members of the Kingdom of Heaven, even though they did not believe, as some did not even to the end, that he who "spake as never man spake" was something more than man.

If we go back to the *ipsissima verba*, so far as we can now get at them, of Christ himself, how much of the doctrine that we are apt to attribute to Christ we shall find to be Pauline—how much more Patristic, Scholastic, Puritan! How little dogma, and how much morality, there is in the Founder of our religion; how few words, and how many works; how little about consequences, how much about motives; in a word, how little theology, and how much religion! I do not of course mean to deny that Moses, Buddha, Christ himself were founders of a theology as well as of a life; I only say that the life came first, since it was that which was most called for by the time, and it was their new views of life which prepared their followers to receive and develop their new views of God. "If any man will *do* his will, he shall know of the doctrine whether it be of God." "He that loveth not his brother whom he hath seen, how can he love God whom he hath not seen?" "Blessed are the pure in *heart*, for they shall see God."

I am aware that distinguished German philosophers, Max Müller among them,* have laid it down that men can not form themselves into a people till they have

---

* "Introduction to the Science of Religion," Lecture III., p. 144–153.

come to an agreement about their religion, and that community of faith is a bond of union more fundamental than any other bond at all. But I do not think that if the distinction which I have drawn between the primeval and the historical religions of the world be kept in sight, there is much necessary antagonism between their view and mine; that a new religion is, in order of time, the outcome and not the cause of a general movement toward a higher life, whether moral or national. Religion is, no doubt, practically all that they say it is—a tie so strong that it can give an ideal unity, as it did in Greece, to tribes differing from one another in degrees of civilization, in interests, and in dialect; but it does not follow that it was historically ever the original moving power in the aggregation of scattered tribes, or that a new religion was at first a revelation of God rather than a revelation of morality. There must have been a previous community of race and language for the religion to work upon; there must also have been a strong, though very possibly an ill-directed and a desultory upheaval of society. The fragments still existing of the primeval creed are no doubt a factor in that upheaval, and feel its force; but the new religion is the result and not the cause of the general movement. It is not till later that it pays the debt it owes to what gave it birth, by lending a higher sanction to each institution of the

new society, and so does in truth become, what philosophers say it is, the most important bond in a national
life. First the aspirations, then that which satisfies
them! First a new conception of the relation of men
to one another, then that conception sanctioned, vivified,
lit up by the newly perceived relation of all alike to
God!

I would also remark that Greece itself, though Max
Müller appeals to it in favor of his own conclusions,
seems to supply an argument in favor of my view. For
even in the Persian wars the common danger and the
common hatred of the " Barbarian " failed to bring about
more than a very transitory coalition between two or
three of the leading states. The ideal unity of the
Greek races was only an ideal, and Panhellenism never
went so far as to unite the different states into a homogeneous people. If there had been a real and spontane-
ous movement among the autonomous cities of Greece
toward centralization, a great reformer might have taken
advantage of it, and working upon the " dim recollection
of the common allegiance they owed from time immemorial to the great Father of Gods and men, the old
Zeus of Dodona, the Panhellenic Zeus,"* have welded
the fragments into a nation. The One would not mere-

---

* "Science of Religion," p. 148.

ly have been dimly discerned behind the Many by the highest minds, but the perception would have been converted into a practical reality. The intellectual mission of Socrates might have taken something of the shape and realized something of the results of the mission of Mohammed. But there was no such national movement in Greece, and therefore no opportunity either for the birth of a new religion or a revival of the old one. In Greek Polytheism we see historically nothing but decay, Mythology having completely overgrown the Religion. The gross stories of Homer and of Hesiod, which so scandalized Socrates and Plato, had, even at that early time, concealed from all but the highest minds the vague primitive belief, common probably to the whole Indo-Germanic race, in one Father who is in Heaven.

To what extent the principle I have laid down as to the origin of the three great historical religions is also true of that of Mohammed will develop itself gradually in the sequel.

It has been remarked, indeed, by writer after writer, that Islam is less interesting than other religions, inasmuch as it is less original. And this is one of the favorite charges brought against it by Christian apologists. In the first place, I am inclined to think that the charge of want of originality, though it can not be denied, has been overdone by recent writers; most conspicuously so by M. Renan, who, ingenious and beautiful as his Essay is, seems disposed to explain the whole fabric of Islamism by the ideas that existed before Mohammed, and the political direction given to it by his successors, most notably by Omar; in fact, it seems to me that the only element left out, or not accounted for, in his analysis of Mohammedanism, is Mohammed himself. His Mohammedanism resembles a Hamlet with not only the Prince of Denmark, but with Shakespeare himself cut out. The disjointed members and some few elements of the fabric remain—about as much as we should have of the Hamlet of Shakespeare in the Amlettus of Saxo-Grammaticus; but the informing, animating, inspiring soul is wanting.

It is undeniable that a vague and hearsay acquaintance with the Old Testament, the Talmud, and the New Testament, and the undefined religious cravings of a few of his immediate predecessors or contemporaries, influenced Mohammed much, and traces of them at second hand may be found in every other page of the Koran; but then, in the second place, it may be asked whether want of originality is any reproach to a religion: for what is religion?

It is that something which, whether it is a collection of shadows projected by the mind itself upon the mirror of the external world, explaining the Macrocosm by the

Microcosm, and invested with a reality which belongs only to the mind that casts them, if indeed even to that, or whether it is indeed an insight of the soul into realities which exist independently of it, and which underlie alike the world of sense and the world of reason; it is something, at all events, which satisfies the spiritual wants of man. Man's spiritual wants, whatever their origin, are his truest wants; and the something which satisfies those wants is the most real of all realities to him.

The founder, therefore, of a religion which is to last must read the spiritual needs of a nation correctly, or at all events must be capable of seeing the direction in which they lead, and the development they will one day take. If he read them correctly, he need not care about any originality beyond that which such insight implies; he will rather do well to avoid it. The religious world was startled a few years ago by the revelations of an Oriental scholar that much supposed to be exclusively the doctrine of the New Testament is to be found in the Talmud, as though some reflection was thereby cast upon the Founder of our religion! Positivists, again, have laid great stress on the fact that some of the moral precepts supposed to be exclusively Christian are to be found in the sacred writings of Confucius and the Buddhists. But what then? Is a religion less true because it recognizes itself in other garbs, because it incorporates

in itself all that is best in the system which it expands
or supplants? What if we found the whole Sermon on
the Mount dispersed about the writings of the Jewish
Rabbis, as we unquestionably find some part of it?
Christ himself was always the first to assert that he
came, not to destroy, but to fulfill. But it is strange
that the avowed relation of Christianity to Judaism has
not protected Islam from the assaults of Christian apologists, grounded on its avowed relation to the two together!

But what of interest, I am free to admit, the religion
of Mohammed loses on the score of originality, it gains
in the greater fullness of our knowledge of its origin.
It is the latest and most historical of the great religions
of the world.

Renan has remarked that the origin of nearly all the
leading phenomena of life and history is obscure. What,
for instance, can Max Müller tell us of the origin of
language? What well-authenticated facts can political
philosophers like Hobbes or Locke, or even scientific
antiquaries like Sir Charles Lyell or Sir John Lubbock,
tell us of the origin of society? What can Darwin tell
us of the origin of life? Trace the genealogy of all existing languages into the three great groups of Aryan,
Semitic, and Turanian; find, if you can, the parent language from which even these three families have originally diverged; are we any nearer an explanation of

what language really is ?   Our hopes, indeed, are aroused
by hints dropped throughout Max Müller's fascinating
book that he has a secret to divulge to those who have
gone through an adequate process of initiation.   But
to our disappointment we find that the explanation of
"Phonetic Types" is only a roundabout way of saying—
what, no doubt, is true — that language is instinctive,
and that we know nothing whatever of its origin.   That
sound expresses thought we knew before; but how does
it express it?   That is the question.   Trace elaborately
through Geological Periods, if you can, the steps by
which the Monad has been developed into Man, and
show that there is no link wanting, and that Nature, so
far as we can trace, never makes a leap.   Perhaps not;
but there is a leap somewhere, and who can say how
vast the leap before the Protoplasm can have received
the something that is not Protoplasm but Life, and which
has all the dignity of life, even though it be a Monad's?

So, too, if the Science of Religion last long enough,
we may one day be able to trace a continuity of growth
from the very dawn of man's belief till, as in history so
in religion,

> "We doubt not through the ages one increasing purpose runs,
>   And the thoughts of men are widened with the process of the suns."

We shall find, however, that, even in the dimmest dawn
of history, the essence of religion was already there, not

forming, but already formed; a feeling of mystery which, as it is the beginning of philosophy, so, perhaps, it is the very first beginning of religion; the distinction between right and wrong; the idea of a Power which is neither Man's nor external Nature's, though it is evidenced by them both; the sense that there is something in this world amiss; and the fear, or, possibly, the hope, that it may be unriddled by and by.* Where did those ideas come from? And do we know any thing more of the origin of religion itself by having traced it to some of its elements?

And what is true of religion generally is also true, unfortunately, of those three religions which I have called, for want of a better name, historical — and of their founders. We know all too little of the first and earliest laborers; too much, perhaps, of those who have entered into their labors. We know less of Zoroaster and Confucius than we do of Solon and Socrates; less

---

* I do not mean to touch here upon the disputed question whether there are races without any definite religious ideas at all. Sir John Lubbock ("Origin of Civilization," cap. iv.) has brought together the testimony of many missionaries and travelers as to a great variety of tribes which seem to be, at all events, without any thing beyond the elements I have named; but I much doubt whether these elements, or some of them, do not exist in all tribes, even in the lowest. It is certain that a longer acquaintance and minuter observation among savage tribes, especially the African, have often led to the reversal of an opinion naturally but hastily formed in the first instance. See Waitz, "Anthropologie der Naturvölker," vol. ii., p. 4.

of Moses and of Buddha than we do of Ambrose and
Augustine. We know indeed some fragments of a frag-
ment of Christ's life; but who can lift the veil of the
thirty years that prepared the way for the three? What
we do know indeed has renovated a third of the world,
and may yet renovate much more; an ideal of life at
once remote and near; possible and impossible; but
how much we do not know! What do we know of his
mother, of his home life, of his early friends, and his
relation to them, of the gradual dawning, or, it may
be, the sudden revelation, of his divine mission? How
many questions about him occur to each of us that must
always remain questions!

But in Mohammedanism every thing is different; here,
instead of the shadowy and the mysterious, we have history.* We know as much of Mohammed as we do even
of Luther and Milton. The mythical, the legendary,
the supernatural is almost wanting in the original Arab
authorities, or at all events can easily be distinguished
from what is historical.† Nobody here is the dupe of

---

- * Cf. Renan, "Études d'Histoire Religieuse," p. 220 and 230.

    † The belief in Jinn, beings created of smokeless fire 2000 years before
Adam, as a part of the original Arab mythology, was not discarded by
Mohammed (Koran, Sura i., 7–8; xlvi.. 28, 29; lvii., 17–18; lxxii., 1,
etc.); but, in other respects, the miraculous and mythological element in
Mohammedanism comes almost exclusively from Persian sources. Persia
has revenged the destruction of her national faith by corrupting in many
particulars the simplicity of the creed of her conquerors. For an exhaust-

himself or of others; there is the full light of day upon all that that light can ever reach at all. "The abysmal depths of personality" indeed are, and must always remain, beyond the reach of any line and plummet of ours. But we know every thing of the external history of Mohammed—his youth, his appearance, his relations, his habits; the first idea and the gradual growth, intermittent though it was, of his great revelation; while for his internal history, after his mission had been proclaimed, we have a book absolutely unique in its origin, in its preservation, and in the chaos of its contents, but on the authenticity of which no one has ever been able to cast a serious doubt. There, if in any book, we have a mirror of one of the master-spirits of the world; often inartistic, incoherent, self-contradictory, dull, but impregnated with a few grand ideas which stand out from the whole; a mind seething with the inspiration pent within it, "intoxicated with God," but full of human weaknesses, from which he never pretended—and it is his lasting glory that he never pretended—to be free.*

---

ive account of Arab ideas on the Jinn, their creation, their influence on human affairs, and their abode, see Note 21 to the Introduction of Lane's edition of "The Thousand and One Nights." The legends illustrating the power of Solomon over the Genii are well known. The notes to Lane's edition of the "Arabian Nights" form a storehouse of accurate information upon Arab manners and customs.

* It was a proverbial saying in very early times among Mussulmans that "Mohammed's character was the Koran."

Upon the striking resemblances between the Koran and the Bible—the book with which it is most naturally compared—and the still more striking differences, I need not now dwell at length, especially as the latter have been admirably drawn out by Dean Stanley.*

To compress, as best I may, into a few sentences what he has said so well, making only a few amendments where, from my point of view, they seem to be called for: The Koran lays claim to a verbal, literal, and mechanical inspiration in every part alike, and is regarded as such by almost all Mohammedans. The Bible makes no such claim, except in one or two controverted passages; and there are few Christians who do not now admit at least a human element in every part of it. The text of the Koran is stereotyped; in the Bible there is an immense variety of readings. The Koran has hitherto proved to be incapable of harmonious translation into other languages; the Bible loses little or nothing in the process. The Bible is the work of a large number of poets, prophets, statesmen, and lawgivers, extending over a vast period of time, and incorporates with itself other and earlier, and often conflicting documents; the Koran comes straight from the brain, sometimes from the ravings, of an unlettered enthusiast, who yet in this proved

---

* "Lectures on the Eastern Church," Lecture VIII., p. 266-273.

KORAN AND BIBLE COMPARED.

himself to be poet and prophet, statesman and lawgiver in one. Finally, the strength of the Koran lies in its uniformity, in its intolerance, in its narrowness; the strength of the Bible in its variety, its toleration, its universality. In all these points, as in the more important one of the morality of its highest revelations, the supremacy of our sacred books over the one sacred book of the Mohammedans is indisputable.

Dean Stanley asks somewhat triumphantly, but on the whole rightly enough, whether there is a single passage in the Koran that can be named, as a proof of inspiration, with St. Paul's description of Charity. But it is worth remarking that a traditional sermon of Mohammed's has been preserved, quoted by Washington Irving,* which, though it is in no way equal to this, the sublimest passage of the greatest of the Apostles, yet shows a real insight into the nature and comprehensiveness of this Christian grace; and may at all events serve as a comment on 1 Corinthians xiii. It is in the form of an Apologue: "When God made the earth, it shook to and fro till he put mountains on it to keep it firm." Then the angels asked, "O God, is there any thing in thy creation stronger than these mountains?" And God replied, "Iron is stronger than the mountains, for it

---

* "Life of Mahomet," p. 87.   He is quoting from Abu Hurairah.

breaks them."—" And is there any thing in thy creation stronger than iron?" "Yes, fire is stronger than iron, for it melts it."—" Is there any thing stronger than fire?" " Yes, water, for it quenches fire."—" Is there any thing stronger than water?" "Yes, wind, for it puts water in motion."—" O our Sustainer! is there any thing in thy creation stronger than wind?" "Yes, a good man giving alms; if he give it with his right hand and conceal it from his left, he overcomes all things." But Mohammed did not end here, or restrict his notion of charity to the somewhat narrow sense which, in common language, it bears now, that of liberal and unostentatious almsgiving: he went on to give almost as wide a definition of charity as St. Paul himself. "Every good act is charity; your smiling in your brother's face; your putting a wanderer in the right road; your giving water to the thirsty, is charity; exhortations to another to do right are charity. A man's true wealth hereafter is the good he has done in this world to his fellow-man. When he dies, people will ask, What property has he left behind him? But the angels will ask, What good deeds has he sent before him?"

But from one point of view the Koran has to the comparative mythologist, and therefore to the student of human nature, an interest quite unique, and not the less absorbing that it springs out of the very defects that

I have pointed out. By studying the Koran, together
with the history of Mohammedanism, we see with our
own eyes, what we can only infer or imagine in other
cases, the precise steps by which a religion naturally and
necessarily develops into a mythology.

In the Koran we have, beyond all doubt, the exact
words of Mohammed without subtraction and without
addition. We see with our own eyes the birth and adolescence of a religion. In the history of Mohammedanism we descry the parasitical growth that fastens on it,
even in its founder's lifetime. We see the way in which
a man who denied that he could work miracles is believed to work them even by his contemporaries, and
how in the next generation the extravagant vision of
the nocturnal flight to the seventh heaven, with all its
gorgeous imagery, and the revolutions of the moon
around the Kaaba, is taken for sober fact, and is propagated with all the elaboration of details which, if they
came from any body, could have come only from Mohammed himself; and yet all of it with the most perfect
good faith. We see how a man, who, though he had once
in an outburst of anger uttered a prophecy which turned
out true, always denied that he could predict the future,
and was yet, in spite of himself, credited with all the supernatural insight of a seer. Lastly, we mark how the
formalities and the sacrifices and the idolatries which

he spent his life in overthrowing, revived in another shape out of the frequency of prayers and fasts that he enjoined, and of the pilgrimages he permitted. The holy places themselves became more holy, as having been the scene of his preaching and of his death, and so in time received more than human honors. We know from history what the outgrowth and superstructure have been, and we read in the Koran how narrow the foundation was.

But from the Bible, by its very nature, and owing to those peculiarities which constitute its special strength, we fail to know, in the same sense, the exact limits of the foundation of the Christendom that has overspread the world. In the outward shape in which it has come down to us, and in the questions connected with the authorship of its different parts and the variety of its contents, the Bible resembles not so much the Koran as the Sonna, which is, of course, rejected by the Sheeah half of the Mohammedan races. Even in the Gospels as we have them, comment and inference, and the individuality of the writer, are mixed with verbal accuracy and exact observation. We can detect conflicting currents of feeling and of thought which it taxes the ingenuity and honesty even of harmonists to harmonize. The New Testament is not less, but more valuable because of these discrepancies. Its undesigned discrepancies have been as valuable in widening the base of our Christianity as its undesigned coincidences are in assuring it. Whether we may legitimately apply the inferences to be drawn from our full knowledge of the growth of Mohammedanism to our imperfect knowledge of the growth of other religions is, of course, open to argument, but the interest and importance of the inquiry can hardly be overestimated.

But over and above the interest attaching to the one religion of the world which is strictly historical in its origin, and which therefore may, rightly or wrongly, be used to explain the origin of those of which we know less, there is the fascination that must always attach to those mixed characters of whom we know so much, and yet so little; who have made the world what it is, and yet whom the world can not read.

> " Hero, impostor, fanatic, priest, or sage :"

which element predominates in the man as a whole we may perhaps discover, and most certainly we can say now it was not the impostor; but taking him at different times and under different circumstances, the more one reads the more one distrusts one's own conclusions, and, as Dean Milman remarks, answers with the Arab, " Allah only knows."*

---

* "Latin Christianity," vol. i., p. 555.

Nor does Mohammedanism lack other claims on our attention. Its ultimate enthusiastic acceptance by the Arabs, the new direction given to it by the later revelations to Mohammed, its rapid conquests, the literature and civilization it brought in its train, the way in which it crumpled up the Roman Empire on one side and the Persian on the other; how it drove Christianity before it on the west and north, and Fire-Worship on the east and south; how it crushed the false prophets that always follow in the wake of a true one, as the jackals do the trail of a lion; how it spread over two continents, and how it settled in a third, and at one time all but overwhelmed the whole, till Charles the Hammer, on the field of Tours, turned it back upon itself; how the indivisible empire, the representative on earth of the Theocracy in heaven, became many empires, with rival Kaliphs at Damascus and Bagdad, at Cairo, Cairoan, and Cordova; how horde after horde of barbarians of the great Turkish or Tartar stock were precipitated on the dominions of the faithful, only to be conquered by the faith of those whose arms they overthrew; how, when the news came that the very birthplace of the Christian faith had fallen into their hands, "a nerve was touched," as Gibbon says, "of exquisite feeling, and the sensation vibrated to the heart of Europe;" how Christendom itself thus became for two hundred years half Mohammedanized, and tried to meet fanaticism by counter-fanaticism — the sword, the Bible, and the Cross against the scimiter, the Koran, and the Crescent; how, lastly, when the tide of aggression had been checked, it once more burst its barriers, and, seating itself on the throne of the Cæsars of the East, threatened more than once the very centre of Christendom — all this is matter of history, at which I can only glance.

And what is its position now ?

It numbers at this day more than one hundred millions, probably one hundred and fifty millions, of believers as sincere, as devout, as true to their creed as are the believers in any creed whatever. It still has its grip on three continents, extending from Morocco to the Malay peninsula, from Zanzibar to the Kirghis horde. It embraces within its ample circumference two extensive empires, one Sonnee, the other Sheeah; the first of which, though it has often been pronounced sick unto death or even dead, is not dead yet, and is even showing signs of reviving vitality. It still grasps the cradles of the Jewish and of the Christian faith, and the spots most dear to both—Mount Sinai and the Cave of Machpelah, the Church of the Nativity and the Church of the Holy Sepulchre. Africa, which had yielded so early to Christianity—nay, which had given birth to Latin Christianity itself; the Africa of Cyprian and Tertullian, of Antony and of Augustine—yielded still more readily to Mohammed; and from the Strait of Gibraltar to the Isthmus of Suez may still be heard the cry which with them is no vain repetition of "Allahu-Akbar"—God is great; there is no god but God, and Mohammed is his prophet.

And if it be said, as it often is, that Mohammedanism has gained nothing since the first flame of religious enthusiasm, fanned, as it then often was, by the lust of conquest, has died out, I answer that this is far from the truth.

In the extreme East, Mohammedanism has since then won and maintained for centuries a moral supremacy in the important Chinese province of Yun-Nan, and has thus actually succeeded in thrusting a wedge between the two great Buddhist empires of Burmah and of China. Within our own memory, indeed, after a fifteen years' war, and under the leadership of Ta Wên Siu— one of those half-military, half-religious geniuses which Islam seems always capable of producing—it succeeded in wresting from the Celestial Empire a territorial supremacy in the western half of this province. Two years ago an embassy of intelligent and, it is worth adding, of progressive and tolerant Mussulmans from Yun-Nan, headed by Prince Hassan, son of the chieftain who has now become the Sultan Soliman, appeared

in England, and the future of the Panthays,* as they
are called, began at length to attract attention, not so
much, I fear, from the extraordinary interest attaching
to their religious history—that interests few Englishmen
—as to the possible opening to our Eastern trade, the
only Gospel which most Englishmen care now to preach,
and one which we did consistently for many years propagate by our commercial wars in China and Japan, at
the expense of every principle of religion and humanity.
Unfortunately the interests of our trade were not sufficiently bound up with the existence of the Panthays to
call for any representations on our part, and Prince
Hassan was compelled to return to Asia without any
prospect of moral support from us or from the Sultan
of Turkey.  On arriving at Rangoon he was met by the
news that the Mussulmans had at length been overpow-
ered by the fearful odds arrayed against them; that
Tali-Fu, the capital, had fallen, and men, women, and
children to the number of some thirty thousand had
been massacred by the victors.  The fate of Momien, the
other stronghold, was of course only a question of time;
but though the short-lived Mohammedan sovereignty
has been destroyed, and what was won by the sword

---

* A name given to them by their Burmese neighbors, from whom the
word has passed into the Western World.  It is said to be a corruption
of the Burmese "Putthee," *i. e.*, Mohammedan.

has since perished by the sword, Mohammedanism itself has not been extinguished in the Celestial Empire.
Within the last eight years that vast tract of country
called Western Chinese Tartary, or Eastern Turkestan,
has thrown off the yoke of China, and has added another
to the list of Mussulman kingdoms.   Khotan and Yark-
and and Kashgar are united under the vigorous rule of
the Atalik Ghazee,* Yakoob Beg.   Whatever may be
his private character, the abolition of the slave-trade
throughout his dominions, his rigid administration of justice, his readiness to establish commercial relations with
India, and the respect shown for Christianity even by
the Meccan pilgrims among his subjects, are some indication of what Mohammedanism may yet have in store
for it in Central Asia under the influence of a master
mind, and with the modifications that are possible or necessary to it.   Throughout the Chinese Empire, at Karachar,
for instance, there are scattered Mussulman communities
who have higher hopes than Buddhism or Confucianism,
and a purer morality than Taoism can supply.   The Pan-

---

* The title was given him by the Ameer of Bokhara.   It means "Guard-
ian of the Champions of Religion."   For the abolition of the slave-trade,
see the best authority on the subject—Shaw's "High Tartary," p. 347;
and for the view of Christians taken by some pilgrims to Mecca from Central Asia, p. 65.   The letters received from Mr. Forsyth's Mission (see
London *Times*, of March 17, 1874) seem quite to bear out the view I had
formed of Yakoob Beg's position.

thays themselves, it is believed, still number a million and a half; and the unity of God and the mission of God's prophet are attested day by day by a continuous line of worshipers from the Atlantic to the Pacific Ocean.

Nay, even beyond, in the East Indian Archipelago, beyond the Strait of Malacca, if I may venture just now so to call it, in Java and Sumatra, in Borneo and Celebes, Islam has raised many of the natives above their former selves, and has long been the dominant faith. It established itself in the Malay Peninsula and Sumatra in the fourteenth, and in Java and Celebes in the fifteenth century; and it is interesting to note, as is remarked by Crawfurd, that about the time it was being gradually expelled from Western Europe, it made up for its expulsion by extending itself to the East of Asia. The Arab missionaries were just in time, for they anticipated by only a few years the first advent of grasping Portuguese and ambitious Spaniards. It can not, of course, be supposed that among races so low in the scale of humanity as are most of the Indian islanders, Mohammedanism would be able to do what it did originally for the Arabs or for the Turkish hordes; but it has done something even for them. It expelled Hindooism from some islands, and a very corrupt Buddhism from others. It was propagated by missionaries who cared very much for the souls they could win, and nothing for the plunder they could carry off. They conciliated the natives, learned their languages, and intermarried with them ; and in the larger islands their success was rapid, and, so far as nature would allow, complete.* The Philippines and the Moluccas, which were conquered by Spain and Portugal respectively, did not become Mohammedan, for they had to surrender at once their liberty and their religion. It is no wonder that the religion known to the natives chiefly through the unblushing rapacity of the Portuguese, and the terrible cruelties of the Dutch, has not extended itself beyond the reach of their swords. Here, as elsewhere in the East, the most fatal hinderance to the spread of Christianity has been the lives of Christians.† I will only add further that the Mussulmans of the East India Islands are very lax in their obedience to many of the precepts of their law, that they are tolerant of other religions, and that the women enjoy a liberty, a position, and an influence which contrasts favorably with that allowed to them in any other Asiatic country.‡

---

* Crawfurd's "Indian Archipelago," vol. ii., p. 275 and 315.

† For the cruelties of the Portuguese, see Crawfurd, vol. ii., p. 403, and for the Dutch, see especially vol. ii., p. 425, seq., and 441. For some startling facts as to the comparative morality of some native and Christian communities in India, see a paper by the Rev. J. N. Thoburn, in the Report of the Allahabad Missionary Conference, held in 1872–73, p. 467–470.

‡ Crawfurd, vol. ii., p. 260 and 269–271 ; and Sir Stamford Raffles's "Java," vol. i., p. 261 ; and vol. ii., p. 2–5.

In Africa, again, Mohammedanism is spreading itself by giant strides almost year by year. Every one knows that within half a century from the Prophet's death the richest states of Africa, and those most accessible to Christianity and to European civilization, were torn away from both by the armies of the faithful, with hardly a struggle or a regret; but few except those who have studied the subject are aware that, ever since then, Mohammedanism has been gradually spreading over the northern half of the continent.

Starting from the northwest corner, it first marched southward from Morocco, and by the time of the Norman Conquest had reached the neighborhood of Timbuctoo, and had got firm hold of the Mandingoes; thence it spread southward again to the Foulahs; and then eastward by the thirteenth century to Lake Tchad, where finally the Arab missionaries from the West joined hands with those from the East in the very heart of Africa.* Of course enormous tracts of heathenism were left, and are still left, in various parts of this vast area, and it is mainly among these that at this day Mohammedan missionaries are meeting every where with a marked success which is denied to our own. We hear of whole tribes laying aside their devil-worship, or immemorial Fetich,

---

* "Anthropologie der Naturvölker," by Dr. Theodor Waitz, p. 248–251.

and springing at a bound, as it were, from the very lowest to one of the highest forms of religious belief. Christian travelers, with every wish to think otherwise, have remarked that the negro who accepts Mohammedanism acquires at once a sense of the dignity of human nature not commonly found even among those who have been brought to accept Christianity.

It is also pertinent to observe here that such progress as any large part of the negro race has hitherto made is in exact proportion to the time that has elapsed, or to the degree of fervor with which they originally embraced or have since clung to Islam. The Mandingoes and the Foulahs are salient instances of this; their unquestionable superiority to other negro tribes is as unquestionably owing to the early hold that Islam got upon them, and to the civilization and culture that it has always encouraged.

Nor can it be said that it is only among those negroes who have never heard any thing of a purer faith that Mohammedanism is making such rapid progress. The Government Blue Books on our West African settlements, and the reports of missionary societies themselves, are quite at one on this head. The Governor of our West African colonies, Mr. Pope Hennessy, remarks that the liberated Africans are always handed over to Christian missionaries for instruction, and that their children are baptized and brought up at the public expense in Christian schools, and are therefore, in a sense, ready-made converts. Yet the total number of professing Christians, 35,000 out of a population of 513,000—very few even of these, as the Governor says, and as we can unfortunately well believe from our experience in countries that are not African, being practical Christians—falls far short of the original number of liberated Africans and their descendants.* On the other hand, the Rev. James Johnson, a native clergyman, and a man of remarkable energy and intelligence as well as of very Catholic spirit, deplores the fact that, of the total number of Mohammedans to be found in Sierra Leone and its neighborhood, three fourths were not born Mohammedans, but have become so by conversion, whether from a nominal Christianity or from Paganism.†

---

* Papers relating to Her Majesty's Colonial Possessions. Part II., 1873, 2d division, p. 14.

† Ibid., p. 15. As Mr. Pope Hennessy's Report has been much criticised, chiefly on the ground that he is a Roman Catholic (see a letter to the London *Times*, of Oct. 21, 1873, signed "Audi alteram partem"), and as I have based some statements upon it, it may be worth mentioning that I have had a conversation with Mr. Johnson, who is a strong Protestant himself, and that he bore testimony to the *bona fides* of the Report, and to its accuracy even on some points which have been most questioned. He told me that Mohammedanism was introduced into Sierra Leone, not many years ago, by three zealous missionaries who came from a great distance. It seems now to be rapidly gaining the ascendency, in spite of all the European influences at work. It may perhaps be questioned, since he does not dwell much upon it, whether Mr. Pope Hennessy, in his re-

And, what is still more to our purpose to remark here, Mohammedanism, as it spreads now, is not attended by some of the drawbacks which accompanied its first introduction into the country. It is spread, not by the sword, but by earnest and simple-minded Arab missionaries. It has also lost, except in certain well-defined districts, much of its intolerant and exclusive character. The two leading doctrines of Mohammedanism, and the general moral precepts of the Koran, are, of course, inculcated every where. But, in other respects, the Mussulman missionaries exhibit a forbearance, a sympathy, and a respect for native customs and prejudices, and even for their more harmless beliefs, which is no doubt one reason of their success, and which our own missionaries and schoolmasters would do well to imitate.

We are assured, on all hands, that the Mussulman population has an almost passionate desire for education; and those in the neighborhood of our colonies would throng our schools, first, if the practical education given were more worth having, and, secondly, if the teachers would refrain from needlessly attacking their cherished and often harmless customs. Wherever Mohammedans are numerous, they establish schools them-

---

marks on the diminished number of Christians in Sierra Leone, made allowance for the return of a certain number of true Christians, such as Bishop Crowther, to their own countries.

selves; and there are not a few who travel extraordinary distances to secure the best possible education. Mr. Pope Hennessy mentions the case of one young Mohammedan negro who is in the habit of purchasing costly books from Trübner in London, and who went to Futah, two hundred and fifty miles away, to obtain an education better than he could find in Sierra Leone itself.* Nor is it an uncommon thing for newly converted Mussulmans to make their way right across the Desert from Bornu, or from Lake Tchad, or down the Nile from Darfour or Wadai, a journey of over one thousand miles, that they may carry on their studies in El-Azhar, the great collegiate Mosque at Cairo, and may thence bring back the results of their training to their native country, and form so many centres of Mohammedan teaching and example.†

Nor as to the effects of Islam when first embraced by a negro tribe can there be any reasonable doubt. Polytheism disappears almost instantaneously; sorcery, with its attendant evils, gradually dies away; human sacrifice becomes a thing of the past. The general moral elevation is most marked; the natives begin for the first

---

* Ibid., p. 10.

† Waitz, p. 251. He calculates the number of students returning each year to be about fifty. To his book, and to the authorities to whom he refers, I owe many of the facts mentioned in the text illustrative of the influence of Islam on the native mind and character.

time in their history to dress, and that neatly. Squalid
filth is replaced by a scrupulous cleanliness; hospitality
becomes a religious duty; drunkenness, instead of the
rule, becomes a comparatively rare exception. Though
polygamy is allowed by the Koran, it is not common
in practice, and, beyond the limits laid down by the
Prophet, incontinence is rare; chastity is looked upon
as one of the highest, and becomes, in fact, one of the
commoner virtues. It is idleness henceforward that
degrades, and industry that elevates, instead of the reverse. Offenses are henceforward measured by a written code instead of the arbitrary caprice of a chieftain
—a step, as every one will admit, of vast importance in
the progress of a tribe. The mosque gives an idea of
architecture at all events higher than any the negro has
yet had. A thirst for literature is created, and that for
works of science and philosophy as well as for commentaries on the Koran.* There are whole tribes, such as
the Jolofs on the River Gambia, and the Haussas, whose
manly qualities we have had occasion to test in Ashan-

---

* Waitz, p. 252–254. Aristotle and Plato are known to not a few
Mohammedans in the interior. Barth, in his "Travels in Central Africa," vol. v., p. 63, mentions that Sidi Mohammed, of Timbuctoo, maintained that they were both Mussulmans—that is to say, worshipers of the
true God. Cf. vol. iii., p. 373, for the case of a Pullo at Massera, who
had read Plato and Aristotle in Arabic, was well acquainted with the history of Spain, and sympathized with the Wahhabees.

tee, which have become to a man Mohammedans, and have raised themselves infinitely in the process; and the very name of Salt-water Mohammedans given to those tribes along the coast who, from admixture with European settlers, have relaxed the severity of the Prophet's laws, is a striking proof of the extent to which the stricter form of the faith prevails in the far interior.

It is melancholy to contrast with these wide-spread beneficial influences of Mohammedanism the little that has been done for Africa till very lately by the Christian nations that have settled in it, and the still narrower limits within which it has been confined. Till a few years ago the good effects produced beyond the immediate territories occupied by them were absolutely nothing. The achievement of Vasco de Gama, for which Te Deums were sung in Europe, proved for centuries to be nothing but the direst curse to Africa. If the oceanic slave-trade has been, to the eternal credit of England in particular, at last abolished by Christian nations, it can not be forgotten that Africa owes also to them its origin, and on the West Coast, at all events, its long continuance. The message that European traders have carried for centuries to Africa has been one of rapacity, of cruelty, and of bad faith. It is a remark of Dr. Livingstone's* that the only art that the natives of

* Livingstone's " Expedition to the Zambesi," p. 240.

Africa have acquired from their five hundred years' acquaintance with the Portuguese has been the art of dis-
tilling spirits from a gun-barrel; and that the only permanent belief they owe to them is the belief that man
may sell his brother man; for this, he says emphatically,
is not a native belief, but is only to be found in the track
of the Portuguese. The stopping of the oceanic slave-
trade by England is an enormous benefit to Africa; but,
if we except the small number of converts made within
the limits of their settlements, it has been the only benefit conferred by Europeans. The extension of African
commerce is of more than doubtful benefit at present.
The chief articles that we export from thence are the
produce of slave-labor, and, what is worse, of a vastly
extended slave-trade, in the inaccessible interior.*

Nor is it wholly without reason that, in spite of Krapf
and Moffat, of Baker, of Frere, and of Livingstone, and
of a score of other single-hearted and energetic philanthropists, the white man is still an object of terror, and
his professed creed an object of suspicion and repug-

---

* For the introduction, or rather the invention, of the slave-trade
by the Portuguese in the year 1444, see Helps's "Spanish Conquest in
America," vol. i., p. 35, seq., and the quotation there given from the
Chronicle of Azurara, relating the capture of two hundred Africans by a
Portuguese company at Lagos, and their shipment to Portugal. A disastrous precedent from that time down to the end of the last century, only
too fatally followed by all the Christian nations of Europe which had the
chance.

nance, to the negro race. Truly, if the question must
be put, whether it is Mohammedan or Christian nations
that have as yet done most for Africa, the answer must
be that it is not the Christian. And if it be asked,
again, not what religion is the purest in itself and
ideally the best—for to this there could be but one answer—but which, under the peculiar circumstances—
historical, geographical, and ethnological—is the religion most likely to get hold on a vast scale of the native mind, and so in some measure to elevate the savage character, the same answer must be returned. The
question is, indeed, already half answered by a glance
at the map of Africa. Mohammedanism has already
leavened almost the whole of Africa to within five degrees of the equator; and, to the south of it, Uganda,
the most civilized state in that part of Central Africa,
has just become Mohammedan.* Last year, a mosque

---

* See some interesting remarks by Mr. Francis Galton at a meeting of
the British Association at Leeds, on Sept. 22, 1873. I have also to thank
him for giving me, in conversation, his experience of Mohammedanism in
Africa, and for directing me to the best authorities on the subject. Along
the coast-line Mohammedanism of a degraded kind has of course extended much farther south, beyond Zanzibar to Mozambique and the Portuguese colonies. There are Mohammedans to be found even among the
Kaffirs and in Madagascar. The original Portuguese settlers found the
Arabs established along the coasts of Mozambique and in the interior.
They exterminated the former; but as they failed to dispossess the latter,
it is possible that some of the *terra incognita* in the interior may be still
Mohammedan.

was built on the shores of the Victoria Nyanza itself, and the Nile, from its source to its mouth, is now, with very few exceptions, a Mohammedan river.

That Mohammedanism may, when mutual misunderstandings are removed, as I hope to show in a future Lecture, be elevated, chastened, purified by Christian influences and a Christian spirit, and that evils such as the slave-trade, which are really foreign to its nature, can be put down by the heroic efforts of Christian philanthropists, I do not doubt; and I can, therefore, look forward, if with something of anxiety, with still more of hope, to what seems the destiny of Africa, that Paganism and Devil-worship will die out, and that the main part of the continent, if it can not become Christian, will become, what is next best to it, Mohammedan.

Anyhow, it is certain that the gains of Mohammedanism, in Africa alone, counterbalance its apparent losses from Russian conquests, and from proselytism every where else; nor can I believe, notwithstanding predictions inspired by the wish, that its work is yet done, or nearly done, in any of the countries that have ever owned its sway.

I speak of the apparent losses from Russian conquest, for the onward march of the Russian Colossus through Central Asia, so far from carrying any form of Christianity with it, seems to intensify the religious convictions of the half-conquered or threatened races. What was dead in the religion before, it revives; to what was only half alive, it gives fresh vigor. Islam has now become with them a patriotism as well as a creed; and Mr. Gifford Palgrave, an able and accurate observer, has lately described how the distinctive precepts of the Mohammedan religion—those enjoining the observance of the month of Ramadhan, the reading of the Koran, the pilgrimage of the Hadj, the abstinence from gaming, from tobacco, and from intoxicating drinks—are now much more rigidly observed in the debatable territories; and, more than this, the Abkhasians with their immemorial antiquity, and the heroic Circassians driven from their homes after a desperate struggle by Muscovite oppression and bad faith, dropping such traces of Christianity as they had, but carrying with them a legacy of immortal hate to the creed and country of their tyrants, have crossed the frontier of the more liberal Turkish Empire, and, coalescing with Koords, Turkomans, and Arabs, have settled down in the uplands of Armenia, and are there forming the nucleus of a new and vigorous and united Mohammedan nation.*

In India, where the two religions are brought face to face, and where, if any where, we may expect the great

---

* Palgrave's "Essays on Eastern Questions," ·iv. and v.

drama to play itself out, Mohammedanism gives no sign of yielding. Unlike Brahmanism, which the thousand influences of Western civilization are sapping in every direction, Mohammedanism, on the contrary, seems to concentrate the strength it already has, and, owing to the efforts of its zealous missionaries, is giving symptoms at once of a Revival and of a Reform that may, at any time, change the religious destinies of the country. The Faithful are as courageous, as sincere, as ardently monotheistic as they ever were; witness it in the Indian Mutiny, the Wahhabee Revival, and the last terrible argument of assassination. The heroism and self-devotion of our missionaries seems to be wasted on them in vain, and except in individual cases I see no sign that it will ever be otherwise. Buddhism and Brahmanism may be driven out of India, but Mohammedanism never, except by the Mohammedan method of the sword.*

Such are the leading facts of Mohammedanism viewed from the outside; and now how are we to account for them?

One thing is certain, that the explanations so readily offered by historians and Christian apologists till within a very recent period will not suffice now. People who think they have nothing to do with a system except to

---

* See Appendix to Lecture I.

attack it, are not those who can best explain the causes of its vitality or its success. One historian tells us that Mohammedanism triumphed by the mere force of arms; another, by the use Mohammed made of the tendency so deeply planted in man to fall victims in masses to any well-conceived imposture; a third traces his success to his skillful plagiarisms from faiths purer than his own; and a fourth to the elevated morality, or to the lax morality, inculcated in the Koran—for both of these are strangely enough urged almost in the same breath by the same people; while, lastly, others dwell on the inherent strength of the founder's character, and the enthusiasm that must accompany a crusade against idolatry.* We feel that most of these have some truth in them, some of them have much; and one or two of them are not only not true, but they are the very reverse of the truth. But we also feel that none of them singly, nor all of them together, adequately account for the phenomena they profess to explain.

In treating of Mohammedanism, as remarked by M. Barthélemy St. Hilaire,† we have to try *in limine* to discard alike our national and our religious prejudices. It was not till Mohammedanism had existed for eight

---

* See some of these explanations admirably dealt with by F. D. Maurice, "Religions of the World," Lecture I.

† "Mahomet et le Koran," Preface, p. 6.

hundred years that it was possible to discard the one, and not till very lately that it was even attempted to discard the other. Since the conquest of Constantinople, or rather since the brilliant naval victory of Don John of Austria at Lepanto, and its final repulse by John Sobieski from the walls of Vienna two hundred and thirty years later, Mohammedanism has ceased, in Europe at least, to be an aggressive and conquering power; and since then it has been possible for the states of Christendom to breathe more freely, and to forget the infidel in the ally or the subject.

Religious prejudice is more difficult to overcome. Men who are ardently attached to their own religion find it difficult to judge another dispassionately, and from a neutral point of view. The philosopher who, according to Gibbon's famous aphorism, looked upon all religions of the Roman Empire as equally false, and the magistrate who looked upon all as equally useful, would be alike incapacitated for viewing the Mussulman creed from the Mussulman stand-point. Perhaps the populace, who looked upon all religions as equally true, would have been the best judge of the three; but I doubt whether in this, as in most epigrammatic sentences, something of truth has not been sacrificed to the antithesis. Nature does not arrange herself in antithetical groups for our convenience; and I doubt whether the mass of any people, at any time, have looked upon all religions as equally true.

But the comparative study of religion is beginning to teach, at all events, the more thoughtful of mankind, not indeed that all religions are equally true or equally elevating, but that all contain some truth; that no religion is exclusively good, none exclusively bad; that any religion which has a real and continued hold on a large body of mankind must satisfy a real spiritual need, and is so far good. God is in all his works, and not the least so in the thoughts and aspirations of his creatures toward himself; and what we have to do is to feel after him in each and all, assured that he is there, even if haply in our ignorance we can find no trace of him.

Truly, when we are dealing with religion at all, even though it be Polytheism or Fetichism, we are " treading upon holy ground ;" and in order that we may treat that creed, sublime in its simplicity, which is our special subject, with that union of candor and of reverence which alone befits it, it is necessary before concluding this introductory Lecture that I should lay down clearly one principle which must guide us in our investigation.

It is this, that for the purposes of scientific investigation, religions must be regarded as differing from one another in degree rather than in kind. This is the one postulate, itself the result of a careful induction, upon which alone the existence of any true science of religion must depend. Without a clear perception of this truth, you enter upon the study of the religions of the world with a preconceived idea, which will color all your conclusions, and will invalidate them the more gravely the more favorable those conclusions are to your own creed. The ordinary distinctions of kind, therefore, drawn between true and false, natural and supernatural, revealed and unrevealed religions are, for our present purpose, unreal and misleading. The fact is that from one point of view all religions are more or less natural, from another all are more or less supernatural; and all alike are to be treated from the same stand-point, and investigated by the same methods. In the Science of Religion, to quote an expression of Max Müller's used in this place, Christianity "owns no prescriptive rights, and claims no immunities." It challenges the freest inquiry; and as it claims to come from God himself, so it fears not the honest use of any faculties that God has given to man. Christianity is indeed a revelation, and what it really reveals is true; and, so far, if the alternative must needs be put in this shape, no Christian would have any doubt in which category to place his own creed.

But does Christianity claim any such monopoly of what is good and true as is implied in this crude classification, or will any one say that there is no real revelation of God in the noble lives of Confucius or Buddha, and no fragments of divine truth in the pure morality of the systems which they founded? Truth, happily for man, is myriad-sided, and happy he who can catch a far-off glance of the one side of it presented to him! Claim, if you like, for the Bible what the Koran does claim for itself and the Bible does not—a rigid or a verbal inspiration. Grant that the truth revealed passed mechanically through the mind of the sacred writer without contamination and without alloy, yet who can say that, since the Verities with which religion deals are all beyond the world of sense, the precise meaning attached by him to any one word in his creed is the same as that attached to it by any other?—*quot homines tot sententiæ.* The recipient subject colors every object of sensation or of thought as it passes into it, and is conscious of that object, not as it entered, but as it has been instantaneously and unconsciously transformed in the alembic of the mind. In religion, as in external nature, the human mind is, as Bacon says, an unequal mirror to the rays of things, mixing its own nature indissolubly with theirs. And this relative element once admitted into religion at all, it follows that to divide religions by an impassable barrier into true and false, natural and revealed, is like dividing music into sacred and secular, and history into sacred and profane. It is a division convenient enough for those—the majority of the human race—who are content with an artificial classification, and who care for no religion but their own; but, for scientific purposes, it is a cross division, it begs the question at issue, and is as unphilosophical as it is misleading.*

Nor do Sacred Books, whatever be the theory of inspiration on which they rest, lend to the religion to which they belong any distinction of kind; they fix the phraseology of a religion, and we are apt to believe that they also fix the thought. They do not do so, however. The "poetic and literary terms thrown out," † to use Mr. Matthew Arnold's happy expression, by the highest minds at the highest objects of thought, as faint approximations only to the truth respecting them, become enshrined in the Sacred Canon. They are misunderstood, or half understood, even by those who hear them from the Psalmist's or the Prophet's own lips, and in a few years the misunderstanding grows till it becomes fixed and rigid.‡ Poetic imagery is mistaken for scientific

---

* For a full discussion of the ordinary methods of classifying religion, see Max Müller's "Science of Religion," p. 123–143.

† "Literature and Dogma," passim; but see especially p. 38–41 and 58.

‡ For admirable illustrations of this, see "Literature and Dogma," cap. ii. and v., p. 123. This part of Mr. Arnold's work, it may be pretty confidently asserted, is done once for all; and its influence will be felt, avowedly or not, throughout the domain of Biblical criticism.

exactness, and dim outlines for exhaustive definitions. A virtue is attached to the words themselves, and the thought, which is the jewel, is hidden by the letter, which is only the casket. If it be true that man never knows how anthropomorphic he himself is, still less do sacred writers know the anthropomorphism and the materialism which will eventually be drawn even from their highest and most spiritual utterances. How little did the author of the prayer at the dedication of the Temple of Solomon—the grandest assertion, perhaps, in the Old Testament of the infinite power and the infinite goodness of God, his nearness to us and his distance from us—imagine that the time would ever come when it would be held that in that Temple alone, and by Jews alone, men could worship the Father!

Christians may and must rise from an impartial study of the religions of the world with their belief vastly deepened that their Sacred Books stand as a whole on a far higher level than other Sacred Books, and that the ideal life of Christianity, while it is capable of including the highest ideals of other creeds, can not itself be attained by any one of them. But the value of this belief will be exactly proportioned to the extent to which they have been able, for the purposes of scientific duty, to divest themselves of any arbitrary assumption in the matter; and they must also acknowl-

edge that it is possible and natural for sincere Mohammedans or Buddhists to arrive at the same conclusions
concerning their own faiths.  It is not easy to be thoroughly convinced of this, or to act upon it; for intolerance is the "natural weed of the human bosom," and
there is no religion which does not seem superstitious
to those who do not believe in it.*

But this belief is far from necessitating in practical
life a religious indifference; nor, however it may seem
so at first sight, is it averse to all missionary efforts.
Missionaries will not cease to exist, nor will they lose
their energy, their enthusiasm, and their self-sacrifice.
But they will go to work in a different way, will view
other religions in a different light, and will test their
success by a different standard.  They will no doubt
be forced to acquiesce in what seems the will of Providence, that a national religion is as much a part of
man's nature as is the genius of his language or the
color of his skin; they will admit that the precise form
of a creed is a matter of prejudice and of circumstance
with most of us, and that, in spite of the rise of historical religions which have shattered other faiths and

---

* See Grote, vol. vi., p. 156, seq., on the death of Socrates.  The boast
of Cicero, "Majores nostri superstitionem a religione separaverunt" (De
Nat. Deorum, ii., 28), is the natural belief of every one, even of the Fetich-
worshiper, concerning his own, and none but his own, creed.

risen upon their ruins, nine tenths of the whole human race have died, and will in all probability continue to die, in the profession of that faith into which they were born; but this will no longer seem to them, as it must seem now, a mysterious and overwhelming victory of evil over good, which appalls the moral sense, and, if a man be not better than the letter of his creed, must tend to shake at once his belief in the universal Father-hood of God and the true brotherhood of humanity; they will rather, in proportion to the strength of their belief in the goodness of God, believe that his creat-ures can not grope after him, even in the dark, without getting that light which is sufficient for them; they will not seek to eradicate wholly any existing national faith, if only it be a living one; nor, as the phrase is, will they aim at "bringing its adherents over to Chris-tianity;" they will seek rather to bring Christianity to them, to infuse a Christian spirit into what is, at worst, not an anti-Christian, but merely a non-Christian, or, it may be, a half-Christian faith.

The Apostles did not cease to be Jews because they became Christians, or to look up to Moses less because they reverenced Christ more. And yet the difference between Judaism and Christianity, between the forms and the ceremonies and the exclusiveness of the one, and the spirituality and the freedom and the universality of the other, is at least as great, as I hope to show, as the difference between a sincere believer in the teachings of the Prophet of Arabia and a humble follower of the character of Christ.

St. Paul, the one model given us in the New Testament of what a missionary should be, in dealing with the faith of a cultivated people much dissimilar to his own—a faith, most people would say now, differing in kind as well as in degree from Christianity—never thought himself of drawing so broad a distinction between the two. He might well have been disposed to do so, for the Polytheism of Athens had long ceased to be an adequate expression of the highest religious life of the people. It was in its decadence even when it had inspired the profoundest utterances of Æschylus or Sophocles; it could not have inspired them then, even had there existed genius like theirs to be inspired. Its oracles were dumb; and yet St. Paul dropped not a word of scorn for the echoes that still lingered and the flames that were still flickering on its shattered altars. He did not talk of false gods or of devil-worship, of imposture or of superstition. Those whom our translation calls "superstitious" he calls "God-fearing." He quotes their great authors with sympathy and with respect. He professes only to give articulate utterance to their own thoughts, and to declare more fully to them that God whom, unknowingly, they already worshiped.

And so, again, in writing to the converts to be found even in the metropolis of the world, and, it must be added, the head-quarters of its vices, while he lashes its moral iniquities and its religious corruptions with an unsparing hand, yet, with a toleration wholly alien to the Jewish race, and without forfeiting his supreme allegiance to his Master, he strikes at the root of the impassable distinction between revealed and unrevealed religion, by pointing out that those who, not having the law, yet did by nature the things contained in the law, were in truth a law unto themselves. He showed that the Eternal could reveal himself as well by his unwritten as by his written law, and that the voice of conscience is, in very truth, to every one who follows it, the voice of the living God.

The missionaries of the future, therefore, will try to penetrate to the common elements which, they will have learned, underlie all religions alike, and make the most of those. They will be able, with a sympathy which is real because it is drawn from a knowledge of the history of their own faith, to point out the abuses which have crept, and always will creep, into an originally spiritual creed. They will inculcate in their teaching and exhibit in their lives, as they do now, something of that highest morality which they have learned from their Master, and which they will then have learned is the very essence of their faith, and which, in its broad outlines at least, in the "secret" as well as in the "method" of Jesus,* may adapt itself to the wants of every nation and every creed.

They will never, therefore, think it necessary to present Christianity to those of an alien creed as a collection of defined yet mysterious doctrines, which must be accepted whole or not at all; but will rather be content to show them Christ himself as he appeared to his earliest disciples — before the mists of metaphysics had gathered around his head, and the watchwords of theology had half hidden him from the view—glorious in his moral beauty, sublime in his self-surrender, divine in his humanity and by reason of it. And they may then leave it to the moral sense of some, at least, in every section of the race, whose greatest glory and Ideal

---

* "Literature and Dogma," p. 343. "Of the all-importance of righteousness there is a knowledge in Mohammedanism, but of the method and secret of Jesus, by which alone is righteousness possible, hardly any sense at all." There is substantial truth in this; but few can read Mr. Arnold's own account of what he conceives the secret and method of Jesus to have been, without feeling that all the higher religions of the world—any religion, in fact, which, controlling the lower part of man's nature and stimulating the higher, makes him to be at peace with himself, which gives hope in adversity, and calmness in the prospect of death —must contain much both of the one and of the other.

Representative he is, to judge of him aright, and to recognize in his person the supreme and the final Revelation of God. Here, in the ambition to set before the eyes of all a higher Ideal, and a more perfect example than any they have yet known; in the proclamation of the truth, which Christ came to proclaim, of the universal Fatherhood, and the perfect love of God—here is ample work for the enthusiasm of humanity; in this sense Christ may live again upon the earth, and in this sense, and only in this, is it likely that Christianity will overspread the world. I have premised this much, even at the risk of anticipating some of the conclusions to which we shall, I believe, ultimately come, because I think it necessary to prevent any misunderstanding as to my point of view.

Ἐξ οἵων οἷος; how far the way was prepared for Mohammed by circumstances, and what part he himself bore in the great revolution that goes by his name; what we are to say on the nature of his mission, on the much-disputed question of his sincerity, of the inconsistencies in his career and the blots upon it, this will form the subject of my next Lecture.

# LECTURE II.

FEBRUARY 21, 1874.

## MOHAMMED.

Μεγάλων ἑαυτὸν ἀξιοῖ ἄξιος ὤν.—ARISTOTLE.

There goeth the son of Abdallah, who hath his conversation in the heavens.—THE KOREISHITES.

A COMPLETE history of the opinions that have been held by Christians about Mohammed and Mohammedanism would not be an uninstructive chapter, however melancholy, in the history of the human mind. To glance for a moment at a few of them.

During the first few centuries of Mohammedanism, Christendom could not afford to criticise or explain; it could only tremble and obey. But when the Saracens had received their first check in the heart of France, the nations which had been flying before them faced around, as a herd of cows will sometimes do when the single dog that has put them to flight is called off; and though they did not yet venture to fight, they could at least calumniate their retreating foe. Drances-like, they could manufacture calumnies and victories at pleasure:

"Quæ tuto tibi magna volant; dum distinet hostem
Agger murorum, nec inundant sanguine fossæ."

The disastrous retreat of Charles the Great through Roncesvalles is turned by romance-mongers and troubadours into a signal victory; Charles, who never went beyond Pannonia, is credited, in the following century, with a successful crusade to the Holy Sepulchre, and even with the sack of Babylon! The age of Christian chivalry had not yet come, and was not to come for two hundred years.

In the romance of "Turpin," quoted by Renan, Mohammed, the fanatical destroyer of all idolatry, is turned himself into an idol of gold, and, under the name of Mawmet, is reported to be the object of worship at Cadiz; and this not even Charles the Great, Charles the Iconoclast, the destroyer of the Irmansul in his own native Germany, would venture to attack from fear of the legion of demons which guarded it. In the song of Roland, the national epic of France, referring to the same events, Mohammed appears with the chief of the Pagan Gods on the one side of him, and the chief of the Devils on the other; a curious anticipation, perhaps, of the view of Satanic inspiration taken by Sir William Muir. Marsilles, Kaliph of Cordova, is supposed to worship him as a god, and his favorite form of adjuration is made to be " By Jupiter, by Mohammed, and by Apollyon"—strange metamorphosis and strange collocation !  Human sacrifices are offered to him, if nowhere else indeed, in the imagination and assertions of Christian writers of the tenth and eleventh centuries, under the various names of Bafum, or Maphomet, or Mawmet; and in the same spirit Malaterra, in his " History of Sicily," describes that island as being, when under Saracenic rule, "a land wholly given to idolatry,"* and the expedition of the Norman Roger Guiscard is characterized as being a crusade against idolatry.  Which people were the greater idolaters, any candid reader of the Italian annalists of this time, collected by Muratori, can say.  It is not a little curious that both the English and French languages still bear witness to the popular misapprehension : the French by the word " Mahomerie ;" the English by the word "mummery," still used for absurd or superstitious rites.†  Nor has a Mohammedan nothing to complain of in the etymology and history, little known or forgotten, of the words "Mammetry"‡ and "Paynim," "termagant"

---

* Bk. ii., p. 1.  "Terram idolis deditam."

† Renan, " Études d'Histoire Religieuse," p. 223, note.

‡ Mammetry, a contraction of Mahometry, used in early English for any false religion, especially for a worship of idols, insomuch that Mam-

and "miscreant;" but to these I can only refer in passing.

In the twelfth century "the god Mawmet passes into the heresiarch Mahomet,"[*] and, as such, of course he occupies a conspicuous place in the "Inferno." Dante places him in his ninth circle among the sowers of religious discord; his companions being Fra Dolcino, a communist of the fourteenth century, and Bertrand de Born, a fighting troubadour: his flesh is torn piecemeal from his limbs by demons, who repeat their round in time to re-open the half-healed wounds. The romances of Baphomet, so common in the fourteenth and fifteenth centuries, attribute any and every crime to him, just as the Athanasians did to Arius. "He is a debauchee, a camel stealer, a cardinal, who, having failed to obtain the object of every cardinal's ambition, invents a new religion to revenge himself on his brethren!"[†]

---

met or Mawmet came to mean an idol. In Shakespeare the name is extended to mean a doll : Juliet, for instance, is called by her father "a whining mammet." See Trench "On Words," p. 112. Paynim = Pagan or Heathen. Termagant, a term applied now only to a brawling woman, was originally one of the names given to the supposed idol of the Mohammedans. Miscreant, originally "a man who believes otherwise," acquired its moral significance from the hatred of the Saracens which accompanied the Crusades. The story of Blue Beard, the associations connected with the name "Mahound," and the dislike of European chivalry in mediæval times for the mare—the favorite animal of the Arabs—are other indications of the same thing.

[*] Renan, loc. cit.                                    [†] Renan, p. 224.

With the leaders of the Reformation, Mohammed, the greatest of all Reformers, meets with little sympathy, and their hatred of him, as perhaps was natural, seems to vary inversely as their knowledge. Luther doubts whether he is not worse than Leo; Melanchthon believes him to be either Gog or Magog, and probably both.* The Reformers did not see that the Papal party, fastening on the hatred of priestcraft and formalism, which was common doubtless to Islam and to Protestantism, would impute to both a common hatred of Christianity, even as the Popes had accused the iconoclastic Emperors of Constantinople eight centuries before.

Now, too, arose the invention—the maliciousness of which was only equaled by its stupidity, but believed by all who wished to believe it—of the dove trained to gather peas placed in the ear of Mohammed,† that people might believe that he was inspired by the Holy Ghost — inspired, it would seem, by the very Being whose separate existence it was the first article of his creed to deny! In the imagination of Biblical commentators later on, and down to this very day, he divides with the Pope the credit or discredit of being

---

* See "Quarterly Review," Art. Islam, by Deutsch, No. 254, p. 296.

† A similar story is told of the great Schamyl; only in this case it is Mohammed himself who takes the form of a dove, and imparts his commands to the hero.

the subject of special prophecy in the books of Daniel
and the Revelation, that magnificent series of tableaux,
a part of which, on the principle that " a prophecy may
mean whatever comes after it," has been tortured into
agreement with each successive act of the drama of history ; while, from another part, lovers of the mysterious
have attempted to cast, and, in spite of disappointment,
will always continue to cast, the horoscope of the future. He is Antichrist, the Man of Sin, the Little Horn,
and I know not what besides ; nor do I think that a
single writer, with the one strange exception of the Jew
Maimonides, till toward the middle of the eighteenth
century, treats of him as otherwise than a rank impostor and a false prophet.

France and England may, perhaps, divide the credit
of having been the first to take a different view, and to
have begun that critical study of Arabian history or literature which, in the hands of Gibbon and of Muir, of
Caussin de Perceval and of St. Hilaire, of Weil and of
Sprenger, has put the materials for a fair and unbiased
judgment within the reach of every one. Most other
writers of the eighteenth century, such as Dean Prid-
eaux and the Abbé Maracci, Boulainvilliers and Voltaire, and some subsequent Bampton lecturers and Arabic professors, have approached the subject only to
prove a thesis. Mohammed was to be either a hero

or an impostor; they have held a brief either for the prosecution or the defense; and from them, therefore, we learn much that has been said about Mohammed, but comparatively little of Mohammed himself.

The founder of the reaction was Gagnier, a Frenchman by birth, but an Englishman by adoption. Educated in Navarre, where he had early shown a mastery of more than one Semitic language, he became Canon of St. Geneviève at Paris; on a sudden he turned Protestant, came to England, and attacked Catholicism with all the zeal of a recent convert. Having been appointed to the Chair of Arabic at Oxford, he proceeded to write a history of Mohammed, founded on the work of Abul Feda, the earliest and most authentic of Arabic historians then known.

The translations of the Koran into two different European languages by Sale and Savary soon followed; and from these works, combined with the vast number of facts contained in Sale's Introductory Discourse, Gibbon, who was not an Arabic scholar himself, drew the materials for his splendid chapter, the most masterly of his "three masterpieces of biography"—Athanasius, Julian, and Mohammed. "He has descended on the subject in the fullness of his strength," has been inspired by it, and has produced a sketch which, in spite of occasional uncalled-for sarcasms and characteristic

inuendoes, must be the delight and despair even of
those who have access, as we now have, thanks especially to Sprenger and Muir, to vast stores of information denied to him. But Gibbon's unfair and unphilo-
sophic treatment of Christianity has, perhaps, prevented
the world from doing justice to his generally fair and
philosophic treatment of Mohammedanism; and, as a
consequence of this, most Englishmen, who do not condemn the Arabian prophet unheard, derive what favorable notions of him they have, not from Gibbon, but
from Carlyle. Make as large deductions as we will on
the score of Carlyle's peculiar views on "Heroes and
Hero-worship," how many of us can recall the shock of
surprise, the epoch in our intellectual and religious life,
when we found that he chose for his "Hero as prophet," not Moses, or Elijah, or Isaiah, but the so-called
impostor Mohammed!

I admitted above that the religion of Mohammed
was in its essence not original. Mohammed never said
it was: he called it a revival of the old one, a return to
the primitive creed of Abraham; and there is reason
to believe that both the great religions of the Eastern
world existing in his time, Sabæanism, that is, and Magianism, had been, in their origin at least, vaguely monotheistic. They had passed through the inevitable stages
of spirituality, misunderstanding, decline, and, lastly, in-

tentional corruption, till the God whom Abraham, according to the well-known Mussulman legend, had been the first to worship, because, while he had made the stars and sun to rise and set, he never rose nor set himself, had withdrawn behind them altogether; the heavenly bodies, from being symbols, had become the thing symbolized; temples were erected in their honor, and idols filled the temples.

And as with Sabæanism, so with Magianism; Ormuzd and Ahriman were no longer the principles brought into existence, or existing, by the permission of the one true God, who, as Zoroaster had taught, would tolerate neither temples nor altars nor symbols; worshiped only on the hill-tops with the eye of faith, quickened though it might be by the glory of the rising or setting sun presented to the bodily eye. Fire had itself become the Divinity; and what offering could be more acceptable to such a God than the human victim, overwhelmed by the mysterious flame, whose divine power he denied?

And combined with these two religions, which had been spiritual in their origin, and, probably, more prominent and popular than either, was the grossest Fetichism—the worship of actual stocks and stones, or of the "grim array" of three hundred and sixty idols in the Kaaba; among which the aerolite—once believed to have been of dazzling whiteness, but long since blackened by the kisses of sinful men—was at once the most ancient and the most sacred.

Nor were Judaism and Christianity themselves unknown in Arabia. The destruction of Jerusalem by Titus had caused a very general migration of Jews from Palestine, southward and eastward, beyond the limits of the Roman Empire, and from that time onward the northern part of Arabia was dotted over by Jewish colonies. In the third century a whole Arabian tribe, even in the south of the Peninsula, had adopted the Jewish faith; and the history of Mohammed proves that the neighborhood of Yathrib* contained many Jewish tribes, which, though they maintained in the land of their exile that proud religious isolation which was their national birthright, were not without their influence on Arab politics.

As to Christianity, it is possible that the very first converts made by St. Paul to the faith which once he had destroyed were of Arab blood.† In the fourth century we hear of Christian churches at Tzafar and at Aden, under the protection of the half-Christianized Himyarite king; and the Abyssinian conquest made a form of Christianity to be the dominant religion, at all

---

* Not called Medina, *i. e.*, Medinat-an-Nabi, "the City of the Prophet," till after the Hegira.

† Epistle to Galatians, i. 17.

events in appearance, in Yemen. But neither of these religions ever struck deep root in the Arabian soil: either the people were not suited to them, or they were not suited to the people. They lived on, on sufferance only, till a faith, which to the Arabs should be the more living one, should sweep them away.

Such were the religious conditions under which Mohammed had to work; and what were the social conditions? Arabia from time immemorial had been split up into a vast number of independent tribes, always at war with one another. The scanty sustenance which an arid soil yielded they were fain to eke out by trading themselves, or by plundering others who conducted caravans along the sea-coast of the Hedjaz, to exchange the spices and precious stones of India or of Hadramaut or of Yemen with the manufactures of Bozra and Damascus. Their hand was against every man, and every man's hand was against them; and a prophecy is hardly needed to explain the fact that an impenetrable country was never penetrated by foreign conquerors. Nor were they as uncivilized as has often been supposed. They were as passionately fond of poetry as they were of war and plunder. What the Olympic Games did for Greece in keeping up the national feeling, as distinct from tribal independence, in giving a brief cessation from hostilities, and acting as a literary centre, that the annual fairs at Okatz and Mujanna were to Arabia. Here tribes made up their dissensions, exchanged prisoners of war, and, most important of all, competed with one another in extempore poetic contests. Even in the "times of ignorance," each tribe produced its own poet-laureate; and the most ready and the best saw his poem transcribed in letters of gold,* or suspended on the wall of the entrance of the Kaaba, where it would be seen by every pilgrim who might visit the most sacred place in the country. There was a wild chivalry, too, about them, a contempt of danger and a sensibility of honor, which lends a charm to all we hear of their loves and their wars, their greed and their hospitality, their rapine and their revenge. The Bedouin has been the same in these respects in all ages. "Be good enough to take off that garment of yours," says the Bedouin robber politely to his victim; "it is wanted by my wife;" and the victim submits, with as good a grace as he can muster, to the somewhat unreasonable demands of a hypothetical lady. El Mutanabi, a poet, prophet, and warrior, three hundred years after the Hegira, but who no doubt had

---

* Called Moállacât. Sprenger and Deutsch agree that this word means, not "suspended," but "strung loosely together," and question the truth of the story of the suspension in the "Kaaba." Some of these poems, as, for instance, that of the poet Labyd, still survive, and are a standing proof of the untaught poetic genius of the Arabs.

his prototypes before it, was journeying with his son
through a country infested by robbers, and proposed to
seek a place of refuge for the night: "Art thou then
that Mutanabi," exclaimed his slave, "who wrote these
lines—

> "'I am known to the night, and the wild and the steed,
> To the guest and the sword, to the paper and the reed?'"

The poet-warrior felt the stain like a wound, and throwing himself down to sleep where he then was, met his
death at the hands of the robbers.* The passion indeed for indiscriminate plunder had, before the time
of Mohammed, so far given way to the growing love
of commerce that a kind of Treuga Dei, or Truce of
God, was observed—in theory at least—during four
months of the year. But what the law forbade then,
*ex hypothesi* it allowed at other times, and it is likely
that the enforced abstention gave at once the zest of
novelty and a clear conscience to the purveyors of the
trade when the four months were over.

Such, very briefly, was the condition of the Arabs
when, to use an expression of Voltaire, quoted by Barthélemy St. Hilaire, "The turn of Arabia" came;† when

* Burton's "Pilgrimage to Mecca," vol. iii., p. 60, where he tells this
story and translates the Arabic lines. See the whole of chap. xxiv. for
a graphic account drawn from personal observation of Bedouin knight-
errantry and poetry and generosity.

† P. 211. See cap. ii., generally, for a description of Pre-Mohammedan
Arabia.

the hour had already struck for the most complete, the most sudden, and the most extraordinary revolution that has ever come over any nation upon earth.

One of the most philosophical of historians has remarked that of all the revolutions which have had a permanent influence upon the civil history of mankind, none could so little be anticipated by human prudence as that effected by the religion of Arabia. And at first sight it must be confessed that the Science of History, if indeed there be such a science, is at a loss to find that sequence of cause and effect which it is the object and the test of all history, which is worthy of the name, to trace out.

The Emperor Justinian, not the least shrewd of the Byzantine emperors, who, some forty years before, had thought it necessary to protect his empire from every possible and from many impossible dangers, had neglected to erect a line of fortresses on the side of his empire which, in defiance of nature, really was the most vulnerable.* "By a precaution which inspired the cowardice it foresaw," he had erected a fortress even at Thermopylæ, where the *religio loci* would rather have called for a Spartan rampart of three hundred men, if only they had been forthcoming. He had kept the

---

* Cf. Gibbon, vol. v., p. 102–111.

Sclavonians out of Constantinople by one long wall, and the Russians out of the Crimea by another; he had fortified Amida and Edessa against the fire-worshipers; had built St. Catharine's, half monastery and half fortress, in the wilderness of Mount Sinai; and had even taken precautions against the savages of Æthiopia: but he had trusted to the six hundred miles of desert which nature had interposed between him and a set of robber tribes, intent only on molesting one another. What hostile force could pass such an obstacle?

But we can see now, and Mohammed himself perhaps saw, that the ground was in many respects prepared for a great social and religious revolution. " It detracts nothing from the fame of a great man to show, so far as we can, how his success was possible."* It is only another proof, if proof were wanting, that genius is little else than insight joined to sustained effort; the eye sees what it brings with it the power of seeing; and the great man differs from his contemporaries chiefly in this, that he can read the dark riddle of his time with an eye a few degrees less obscured than those around him. He is the greatest product of his age, but he is still its product, and he is only the father of the age that is to succeed in so far as he owns his parent-

---

* M. Barthélemy St. Hilaire, " Mahomet et le Koran," p. 51.

age. He marches indeed in front of his age; but his influence will be permanent or fleeting precisely so far as he discerns the direction in which it would advance at a slower pace without him.* When he tries to go beyond this, and to force the world out of its groove to adopt hobbies of his own, then begins the region of the remote, the selfish, the personal; in this the great man fails, and hence the commonplaces on the failure of greatness, and the greatness of failure, with which we are all familiar. "Perish my name," said Danton, "but let the cause triumph;"† and personal failure of this kind is to the great man no failure at all—it is only another word for success. The truth is that greatness, so far as it is the truest greatness, rarely fails altogether of its object; and that failure is great only when the end proposed is good, and the human means, though inadequate to its attainment, are yet a real advance toward it.

It must be remembered therefore as regards what seems the sudden birth of the Arabian nation, fully armed, like Athena from the head of Zeus, that the annual resort to Mecca for purposes of trade, poetry,

---

* Cf. Guizot's "Lectures on History," vol. iii., lect. xx.; and Mill's Review of them in "Dissertations and Discussions," vol. ii., p. 249, 250.

† A similar saying is attributed to Cavour: "Perish my name and memory, so that Italy be made a nation!"

and religion, had pointed to the Holy City as to a possible metropolis; and to the Koreishites, the hereditary guardians of the Kaaba, as the potential rulers of a future people; while, as regards the new religion, there was the groundwork of Monotheism underlying all the abuses and corruption of Magianism and Sabæanism. There was also a class of people, called Hanyfs, who prided themselves on preserving the original creed of Abraham, and even his sacred books; while Ibn-Ishac,* the earliest-known historian of Islam, records a meeting of four or five among the Koreishites at which it was

---

* He died A.H. 151. His work has been preserved for us in the Sirat-er-racoul of Ibn-Hisham, who died in the year of the Hegira 213. The fullest and most trustworthy historian, in the judgment of Muir and Sprenger, whose writings have come down to us, is the Katib al Wakidy, or secretary of the historian Wakidy : died A.H. 207. The MS. was discovered by Sprenger at Cawnpore. Among other discoveries of Sprenger may be mentioned a portion of the biography of Mohammed by Tabari, who died A.H. 310, and a complete biographical dictionary, termed Içaba, of the companions of Mohammed, compiled by Ibn-Hidjr, in the fifth century, from writers, whose names he gives, of earlier and incontestable authority. It contains the biographies of some 8000 people. And it may be hoped that the government of India, which numbers among its subjects more than thirty million Mussulmans, may recognize, if they have not already done so, the imperial importance of publishing the three remaining folios of the work. Sprenger brought out one volume, but an order of the Court of Directors suspended the publication of the rest. See Sprenger, Preface, p. 12, where it may be observed how modestly he passes over his own great discoveries, and does not even allude to the slight shown the work by the Directors. Learned and critical Mohammedans, it would seem, do not think so highly of Wakidy and his secretary as Muir and Sprenger do; they prefer Ibn-Hisham. See Muir, vol. i., p. 77–105.

resolved to open a crusade against idolatry, and to seek for the original and only true faith; and they straightway abandoned their homes and spread over the world in the quest of this Holy Grail.*

Mohammedanism therefore is no real exception to the principle I have laid down above as to the origin of the Historical Religions of the world, though, at first sight, it may appear to be so. To Mohammed's own mind it is quite true that the theological element was the predominant and inspiring one, but Mohammed's mind itself was the outcome, at least as much as it was the cause, of the great revolution which goes by his name. There was a general social and religious upheaving at the head of which the Prophet placed himself, and which partly carried him on with it, partly he himself carried it on; the train was already laid, and the spark from heaven was all that was needed to set the Arab world ablaze. In this sense it is perhaps true, as Renan has remarked and the Koran itself declares, that Mohammedanism was preached before the time of Mohammed; but there were Mohammedans before Mohammed only in the sense in which there were Zoroastrians before Zoroaster, Lutherans before Luther, and Christians before Christ. Renan has himself re-

---

* Sprenger, p. 81. These four "inquirers" were Waraka, Othman, Abayd, and Zayd.

marked elsewhere, though he seems to have forgotten it in dealing with Mohammedanism, that the glory of a religion belongs to its founder, and not to his predecessors or to his successors.* It is easy, he says himself, to try to awake faith, and it is easy to be possessed by it when once it has been awakened; but it is not easy to inspire it. It is the grandest gift, a very gift of God.

But though, as I have said, the hour had come, the youth of Mohammed gave few signs that he was the man. The portents which ushered in his birth, and that attended his early youth, are the offspring of an-

---

* It seems to me, though I would speak with the utmost diffidence in venturing to dissent from the greatest European authority on the subject, that Sprenger errs in the same direction as Renan when he says in his volume, published at Allahabad (p. 171), that Abu Bakr did more for the success of Islam than the Prophet himself; and again (p. 174). after enumerating all those who, merely from their vague Monotheism, he calls the predecessors of Mohammed, he says that even after Mohammed was acknowledged as the messenger of God, Omar had more influence on the development of the Islam than Mohammed himself. "The Islam is not the work of Mohammed; it is not the doctrine of the impostor . . . it is the offspring of the spirit of the time, and the voice of the Arabic nation. . . . There is, however, no doubt that the impostor has defiled it by his immorality and perverseness of mind." It is fair to say that this tone seems somewhat moderated, or even altered in the author's subsequent and greater work. Cf., however, vol. ii., p. 83–88. One is inclined to ask, if Islam was merely the spirit of the time, who proved himself best able to read that spirit? Was it Abu Bakr and Omar, or was it Mohammed that produced the Koran? And is it their personality, or his, which has stamped itself with ineffaceable clearness for all time upon the Eastern world?

other country and of a later age. The celestial light
that beamed in the sky and from his newly opened
eyes; the Tigris overflowing its banks; the palace of
Chosroes toppling over to the ground; the sacred fire
of Zoroaster, which had burned for one thousand
years, suddenly extinguished; the mules that talked
and the sheep that bowed to him, were unknown to the
contemporaries of Mohammed, and Mohammed himself says nothing of them! He was a man of few
words, and he had few friends: notable chiefly for
his truthfulness and good faith, they called him "Al
Amyn," the Trusty. His tending his employer's flocks;
his journeys to Syria; possibly his short-lived friendship there with Sergius or Bahira, a Nestorian monk;
his famous vow to succor the oppressed; his employment by Kadijah in a trade venture, and his subsequent happy marriage with her, are about the only
noteworthy external incidents in his early life.

Up to the age of forty there is nothing to show that
any serious scruple had occurred to him individually
as to the worship of idols, and in particular of the
Black Stone, of which his family were the hereditary
guardians. The sacred month of Ramadhan, like other
religious Arabs, he observed with punctilious devotion;
and he would often retire to the caverns of Mount Hira
for purposes of solitude, meditation, and prayer. He

was melancholic in temperament, to begin with; he
was also subject to epileptic fits, upon which Sprenger
has laid great stress, and described most minutely,* and
which, whether under the name of the "sacred disease"
among the Greeks, or "possession by the devil" among
the Jews, has in most ages and countries been looked
upon as something specially mysterious or supernatural.   It is possible that his interviews with Nestorian
monks, with Zeid, or with his wife's cousin Waraka,
may have turned his thoughts into the precise direction they took.   Dejection alternated with excitement;
these gave place to ecstasy or dreams; and in a dream,
or trance, or fit, he saw an angel in human form, but
flooded with celestial light, and displaying a silver roll.
"Read!" said the angel.   "I can not read," said Mohammed.   The injunction and the answer were twice
repeated.†   "Read," at last said the angel, "in the

---

* Sprenger, vol. i., cap. iii., p. 207.   He thinks Mohammed suffered
from hysteria, followed by catalepsy, rather than epilepsy; for the Prophet
does not seem to have lost all consciousness.   It is worth remarking that
Sprenger's medical knowledge is not very favorable in its result to Mohammed.   He starts by saying, p. 210, that all hysterical people have a
tendency to lying and deceit.   This is his major premise.   His minor is
that Mohammed was hysterical, and the inference is obvious.   Accordingly, we are not surprised to find him (vol. i., cap. iv., p. 306, note)
speaking of the "*vision*" of the flight to Jerusalem as one "lie," and
that to the seventh heaven as another lie.

† Cf. Sura xcvi.   Deutsch (Islam, p. 306) renders the word usually
translated "Read" by "Cry," comparing Isaiah xi. 6.

name of the Lord, who created man out of a clot of
blood; read, in the name of the Most High, who taught
man the use of the pen, who sheds on his soul the ray
of knowledge, and teaches him what before he knew
not." Upon this Mohammed felt the heavenly inspiration, and read the decrees of God, which he afterward
promulgated in the Koran. Then came the announce-
ment, "O Mohammed, of a truth thou art the Prophet
of God, and I am his angel Gabriel."*

This was the crisis of Mohammed's life. It was
his call to renounce idolatry, and to take the office of
Prophet. Like Isaiah, he could not at first believe
that so unworthy an instrument could be chosen for

---

* Strangely enough, Sir William Muir, vol. ii., p. 89–96, selects this
period, above all others in Mohammed's life, as the one in which to suggest his peculiar view that the Prophet's belief in his inspiration was Satanic in its origin; and he supports his view by a somewhat elaborate
parallel with the temptations which presented themselves to Christ at the
beginning of his work. Whether such a *Deus ex machinâ* is required to
untie the knot is hardly within my province to inquire, since the whole
matter is alike incapable of proof and disproof; but it seems pertinent to
remark, first, that the developed and quasi-scientific conception of such a
being as Sir William Muir pictures is Persian rather than Jewish in its
origin, and is found in Palestine only after the Captivity; and, secondly, that if the spirit of evil did suggest the idea to Mohammed, he never
so completely outwitted himself, since friend and foe must alike admit
that it was Mohammed's firm belief in supernatural guidance that lay
at the root of all he achieved. Without this we should never have
heard of him except as one of a thousand short-lived Arabian sectaries;
with it he created a nation, and revivified a third of the then known
world.

such a purpose. "Woe is me, for I am undone, because I am a man of unclean lips, and I dwell in the midst of a people of unclean lips;" but the live coal was not immediately taken from the altar and laid upon his, as upon Isaiah's lips. Trembling and agitated, Mohammed tottered to Kadijah and told her his vision and his agony of mind. He had always hated and despised soothsayers, and now, in the irony of destiny, it would appear that he was to become a soothsayer himself. "Fear not, for joyful tidings dost thou bring," exclaimed Kadijah. "I will henceforth regard thee as the prophet of our nation." "Rejoice," she added, seeing him still cast down; "Allah will not suffer thee to fall to shame. Hast thou not been loving to thy kinsfolk, kind to thy neighbors, charitable to the poor, faithful to thy word, and ever a defender of the truth?" First the life, and then the theology, in the individual as in the tribe and the nation.

But the assurances of the good Kadijah, and the conversions of Zeid and Waraka, did not bring the live coal from the altar. A long period of hesitation, doubt, preparation followed. At one time Mohammed even contemplated suicide, and he was only restrained by an unseen hand, as he might well call the bright vision of the future, pictured in one of the earliest Suras of the

Koran,* when the help of God should come and victory, when he "should see the people crowding into the
one true Faith, and he, the Prophet, should celebrate
the praise of his Lord, and ask pardon of him, for
he is forgiving." Three years, the period of the Fatrah, saw only fourteen proselytes attach themselves to
him. His teaching seemed to make no way beyond
the very limited circle of his earliest followers. His rising hopes were crushed. People pointed the finger of
scorn at him as he passed by : " There goeth the son
of Abdallah, who hath his converse with the heavens !"
They called him a driveler, a star-gazer, a maniac-poet.
His uncles sneered, and the main body of the citizens
treated him with that contemptuous indifference which
must have been harder to him to bear than active per-
secution. Well might he, to take an illustration suggested by Sir W. Muir himself,† like Elijah of old,
go a day's journey into the wilderness, and request for
himself that he might die, and say, " It is enough, O
Lord ; now take away my life, for I am not better than
my fathers ;" or, again, " I have been very jealous for
the Lord God of hosts, because the people have forsaken thy covenant, thrown down thine altars, and
slain thy prophets with the sword ; and I, even I,

---

* Sura cx.                         † Muir, vol. ii., p. 228.

only am left, and they seek my life to take it away."
At times his distress was insupportable :

> "And had not his poor heart
> Spoken with That, which, being every where,
> Lets none who speaks with Him seem all alone,
> Surely the man had died of solitude."

But out of weakness came forth strength at last; out
of doubt, certainty; out of humiliation, victory. Another vision, in which he was commanded to preach
publicly, followed ; and now he called the Koreishites
of the line of Hachim together, those who had most to
lose and least to gain by his reform, and boldly an-
nounced his mission. They tried persuasion, entreaties,
bribes, and threats. " Should they array against me
the sun on my right hand, and the moon on my left,"
said Mohammed, " yet while God should command me,
I would not renounce my purpose." These are not the
words, nor this the course, of an impostor.

Ten more years passed away; his doctrine fought its
way amid the greatest discouragements and dangers
by purely moral means, by its own inherent strength.
Kadijah was dead; Abu Taleb, his uncle and protector,
died also. Most of Mohammed's disciples had taken
refuge in Abyssinia, and at last Mohammed himself was
driven to fly for his life with one companion, his early
convert, Abu Bakr. For three days he lay concealed in
a cavern, a league from Mecca. The Koreishite pur-

suers scoured the country, thirsting for his blood. They approached the cavern. "We are only two," said his trembling companion. "There is a third," said Mohammed; "it is God himself." The Koreishites reached the cave; a spider, we are told, had woven its web across the mouth, and a pigeon was sitting on its nest in seemingly undisturbed repose. The Koreishites retreated, for it was evident the solitude of the place was unviolated; and, by a sound instinct, one of the sublimest stories in all history has been made the era of Mohammedan Chronology.

It is unnecessary to follow connectedly and in detail any other incidents in Mohammed's life. The above may be found, with some variety in the details, in any History of Mohammed,* but I have thought it essential to dwell upon them, however familiar they may be to some of us, as they seem to me, apart from their own intrinsic beauty, to supply the key to almost every thing else in Mohammed's career.

The question of the sincerity of Mohammed has been much debated; but to me, I must confess, that to question his sincerity at starting, and to admit the above indisputable facts, is very like a contradiction in terms. Nor could any one have done what Mohammed did without

---

* See especially Washington Irving, p. 32, 33; and Muir, vol. ii.

the most profound faith in the reality and goodness of his cause.   Fairly considered, there is no single trait in his character up to the time of the Hegira which calumny itself could couple with imposture: on the contrary, there is every thing to prove the real enthusiast arriving slowly and painfully at what he believed to be the truth.

It has been remarked by Gibbon that no incipient prophet ever passed through so severe an ordeal as Mohammed, since he first presented himself as a prophet to those who were most conversant with his infirmities as a man.  Those who knew him best—his wife, his eccentric slave, his cousin, his earliest friend, he who, as Mohammed said, alone of his converts, " turned not back, neither was perplexed "—were the first to recognize his mission.   The ordinary lot of a prophet was in his case reversed; he was not without honor save among those who did not know him well.   Strange that Voltaire, who himself wrote on Mohammed, and even made him the subject of a drama, should, with Mohammed's example before him, have ventured on his immoral paradox that " No man is a hero to his valet."   Explained in one sense, that a small mind can not fully understand or appreciate a great one, it is a feeble truism; explained in another, which was the sense Voltaire meant, that the hero is only a hero to those who see him at a distance, and that there is no such thing as true greatness, it is an audacious falsehood.  It is almost equally strange that Gibbon, who has done such full justice to Mohammed in the general result, should say at starting, " Mohammed's religion consists of an eternal truth and a necessary fiction—There is one God, and Mohammed is his Prophet." It was, as I have endeavored to show, no fiction to Mohammed himself or to his followers; had it been so, Mohammedanism could never have risen as it did, nor be what it is now.

But before we go on to consider those points in Mohammed's career which are really open to question, it may be well to recall a few prominent characteristics of the man who has stamped his impress so deeply on the Oriental world.  Minute accounts of his appearance and of his daily life have been preserved to us; they may be found in most of the biographies, and Sir William Muir in particular has given us copious extracts from the writings of the secretary of Wakidy.*

Mohammed was of middle height and of a strongly built frame; his head was large, and across his ample forehead, and above finely arching eyebrows, ran a strongly marked vein, which, when he was angry, would turn black and throb visibly.  His eyes were coal-black, and piercing in their brightness; his hair curled slightly;

* Muir, vol. iv., Supplement to Chap. XXXVII.; cf. also Deutsch's " Islam," p. 302–304.

and a long beard, which, like other Orientals, he would stroke when in deep thought, added to the general impressiveness of his appearance. His step was quick and firm, "like that of one descending a hill." Between his shoulders was the famous mark, the size of a pigeon's egg, which his disciples persisted in believing to be the sign of his prophetic office; while the light which kindled in his eye, like that which flashed from the precious stones in the breastplate of the High-Priest, they called the light of prophecy.

In his intercourse with others, he would sit silent among his companions for a long time together; but truly his silence was more eloquent than other men's speech, for the moment speech was called for, it was forthcoming in the shape of some weighty apothegm or proverb, such as the Arabs love to hear. When he laughed, he laughed heartily, shaking his sides and showing his teeth, which "looked as if they were hailstones." He was easy of approach to all who wished to see him, even as "the river-bank to him that draweth water therefrom." He was fond of animals, and they, as is often the case, were fond of him. He seldom passed a group of children playing together without a few kind words to them; and he was never the first to withdraw his hand from the grasp of one who offered him his. If the warmth of his attachment may be measured, as in fact it may, by the depth of his friends' devotion to him, no truer friend than Mohammed ever lived. Around him, in quite early days, gathered what was best and noblest in Mecca; and in no single instance, through all the vicissitudes of his checkered life, was the friendship then formed ever broken. He wept like a child over the death of his faithful servant Zeid. He visited his mother's tomb some fifty years after her death, and he wept there because he believed that God had forbidden him to pray for her. He was naturally shy and retiring: "as bashful," said Ayesha, "as a veiled virgin." He was kind and forgiving to all. "I served him from the time I was eight years old," said his servant Anas, "and he never scolded me for any thing, though I spoiled much." The most noteworthy of his external characteristics was a sweet gravity and a quiet dignity, which drew involuntary respect, and which was the best, and often the only protection he enjoyed from insult.

His ordinary dress was plain, even to coarseness; yet he was fastidious in arranging it to the best advantage. He was fond of ablutions, and fonder still of perfumes; and he prided himself on the neatness of his hair and the pearly whiteness of his teeth. His life was simple in all its details. He lived with his wives in a row of humble cottages, separated from one another by palm branches, cemented together with mud. He would kindle the fire, sweep the floor, and milk the goats himself. Ayesha tells us that he slept upon a leathern mat, and that he mended his clothes, and even clouted his shoes, with his own hand. For months together, Ayesha is also our authority for saying that he did not get a sufficient meal. The little food that he had was always shared with those who dropped in to partake of it. Indeed, outside the Prophet's house was a bench or gallery, on which were always to be found a number of the poor who lived entirely on the Prophet's generosity, and were hence called the "people of the bench." His ordinary food was dates and water, or barley bread; milk and honey were luxuries of which he was fond, but which he rarely allowed himself. The fare of the desert seemed most congenial to him, even when he was sovereign of Arabia. One day some people passed by him with a basket of berries from one of the desert shrubs. " Pick me out," he said to his companion, " the blackest of those berries, for they are sweet—even such as I was wont to gather when I fed the flocks of Mecca at Adgad."

Such were some of the characteristics of the man whom the Arabs were now called upon to recognize as the prophet of their country, and as a messenger direct from God.

Monotheism, pure and simple, if it is to be a life as well as a creed, almost postulates the prophetic office.

The Creator is at too great a distance from his creatures to allow of a sufficiently direct communication with them. The power, the knowledge, the infinity of God overshadow his providence, his sympathy, and his love. Renan has remarked that in only two ways can such a gap be bridged over: first, if, as in the Indian Avatar, from time to time, or, as in Christianity, once for all, there is an actual manifestation of the Godhead upon earth; or, secondly, if, as in Judaism or in Buddhism, the Deity chooses a favored mortal, who may give to his brother men a fuller knowledge of the divine mind and will.* The latter would seem the form most congenial to the Semitic mind, if one may be allowed to use that convenient but, since the bold generalizations in which Renan has indulged respecting them, somewhat misleading word. The Arabs themselves looked up to Adam, Noah, Abraham, and Moses as prophets; Mohammed did the same, and added Christ to their number. He held that each successive revelation had been higher than the preceding one, though each was complete in itself, as being adequate to the circumstances of the time. Was there, Mohammed might ask, any reason to suppose that Christ had been the last of the prophets, and that his revelation was absolutely as well as relatively final; and

---

* Renan, p. 278.

were there not evils enough in Arabia and in the world to call for a further communication from heaven? To say that Arabia needed renovation was to say in other words that the time for a new prophet had come, and why might not that prophet be Mohammed himself? Sprenger, the most recent and exhaustive writer on the subject, has shown that for some hundred years before Mohammed the advent of another prophet had been expected and even predicted. So strong was the general conviction on the subject that the Arab tribes were guided by it even in their politics.*

But, if we admit the sincerity of Mohammed and the naturalness of his belief up to the time of the Hegira, what are we to say of him during his first years of exile at Medina, and again of his subsequent successes?

It is unquestionably true that a change does seem to come over him. The revelations of the Koran are more and more suited to the particular circumstances and caprices of the moment. They are often of the nature of political bulletins or of personal apologies, rather than of messages direct from God. Now appears for the first time the convenient but dangerous doctrine of ab-

* Sprenger, vol. i., p. 245, quotes a saying of the Arabs that the children of Shem are prophets, of Japhet kings, of Ham slaves. We are told that the Arab women were at this time in the habit of praying for male children, in the hope that of them the long-expected prophet might be born.

rogation, by which a subsequent revelation might super-
sede a previous one.*

The limitation to the unbounded license of Oriental
polygamy which he had himself imposed, he relaxes in
his own behalf: † the greatest stain, and an indelible
one, on his memory, though it is possible that he may
have justified himself to his own mind by the Ethiopian
marriage not condemned in the case of Moses.‡ The
public opinion even of the harem was scandalized by
his marriage with Mary, an Egyptian, a Christian, and a
slave. His marriage with Zeinab, the wife of Zeid, his
freedman and adopted son, divorced as she was by Zeid
for the express purpose that Mohammed might marry
her, was still worse. It was felt as an outrage even
upon the lax morality of an Oriental nation, till all rec-
lamations were hushed into silence by a Sura of the
Koran which rebuked Mohammed, not for his laxity,
but for his undue abstinence !§

---

* Sura xvi., 103 ; ii., 100.

† Sura xxxiii., 49 ; lxvi., 1.

‡ See Lecture IV., p. 210.

§ Sura xxxiii., 37.  See a good passage on the subject in the *British
Quarterly Review* for January, 1872, p. 131.

It should be remembered, however, that most of Mohammed's marriages are to be explained at least as much by his pity for the forlorn
condition of the persons concerned as by other motives.  They were almost all of them with widows who were not remarkable either for their
beauty or their wealth, but quite the reverse.  May not this fact, and

The doctrine of toleration gradually becomes one of extermination; persecuted no longer, he becomes a persecutor himself; with the Koran in one hand, the scimiter in the other, he goes forth to offer to the nations the threefold alternative of conversion, tribute, death. He is once or twice untrue to the kind and forgiving disposition of his best nature; and is once or twice unrelenting in the punishment of his personal enemies, especially of the Jews, who had disappointed his expectation that they would join him, and of such as had stung him by their lampoons or libels. He is even guilty more than once of conniving at the assassination of inveterate opponents; and the massacre of the Bani Koreitza, though they had deserted him almost on the field of battle, and their lives were forfeit by all the laws of war, moved the misgivings of others than the disaffected. He might, no doubt, believing, as he did, in his own inspiration, have found an ample precedent for the act in the slaughter of the Canaanites by Joshua two thousand years before, or even in the wars of Saul and David with neighboring tribes; but, judged by any but an Oriental standard of morality, and by his own con-

---

his undoubted faithfulness to Kadijah till her dying day, and till he himself was fifty years of age, give us some ground to hope that calumny has been at work in the story of Zeinab? There are some indications on the face of it that this is the case.

spicuous magnanimity on other occasions, his act, in all its accessories, was one of cold-blooded and inhuman atrocity.

Can we explain away or extenuate these blots on his memory, or, if we can not, are they inconsistent with substantial sincerity and single-mindedness? Here is a problem of surpassing interest to the psychologist, and I have only time to touch lightly upon it.

In the first place, the change in his character and aims is not to be separated from the general conditions of his life. At first he was a religious and moral reformer only, and could not, even if he would, have met the evils of his time by any other than by moral means. If he was without the advantages, he was also free from the dangers, of success. A religion militant is, as all ecclesiastical history shows, very different from a religion triumphant. The Prophet in spite of himself became, by the force of circumstances, more than a prophet. Not, indeed, that with him height ever begot high thoughts. He preserved to the end of his career that modesty and simplicity of life which is the crowning beauty of his character; but he became a temporal ruler, and, where the Koran did not make its way unaided, the civil magistrate naturally used temporal means. Under such circumstances, and when his followers pressed upon him their belief in the nature of his mission, who can draw the line where enthusiasm ends and self-deception or even imposture begins? No one who knows human nature will deny that the two are often perfectly consistent with each other. Once persuaded fully of his divine mission as a whole, a man unconsciously begins to invest his personal fancies and desires with a like sanction: it is not that he tampers with his conscience; he rather subjects conscience and reason, appetite and affection, to the one dominating influence; and so, as time goes on, with perfect good faith gets to confound what comes from below with what comes from above. What is the meaning of the term "pious frauds," except that such acts are frauds in the eyes of others, acts of piety in the eyes of the doer? The more fully convinced a man is of the goodness of his cause, the more likely is he to forget the means in the end; he need not consciously assert that the end justifies the means, but his eyes are so fixed upon the end that they overlook the interval between the idea and its realization. He has to maintain a hold over the motley mass of followers that his mission has gathered around him. Must he not become all things to all to meet their several wants? Perhaps he does become so, and, in the process, what he gains in the bulk of his influence he loses in its quality. Its intensity is in inverse proportion to its extension. No man — I quote here, with only such slight alteration as adapts them to my subject, the noble words of George Eliot: "No man, whether prophet, statesman, or popular preacher, ever yet kept a prolonged hold over a mixed multitude without being in some measure degraded thereby. His teaching or his life must be accommodated to the average wants of his hearers, and not to his own finest insight. But, after all, we should regard the life of every great man as a drama, in which there must be important inward modifications accompanying the outward changes."* Rigid consistency in itself is no great merit —rather the reverse: what one has a right to demand in a great man is that the intensity of the central truth he has to deliver should become, not less, but more intense; that that flame shall burn so clear as to throw into the shade other objects which shine with a less brilliant light; that the essence shall be pure even if some of the surroundings be alloyed; and this, I think, if not more than this, with all his faults, we may affirm of Mohammed.

On the whole the wonder is to me not how much, but how little, under different circumstances, Mohammed differed from himself. In the shepherd of the desert, in the Syrian trader, in the solitary of Mount Hira, in

---

* "Romola," ch. xxv., p. 214—American edition.

the reformer in the minority of one, in the exile of Medina, in the acknowledged conqueror, in the equal of the Persian Chosroes and the Greek Heraclius, we can still trace a substantial unity. I doubt whether any other man, whose external conditions changed so much, ever himself changed less to meet them : the accidents are changed, the essence seems to me to be the same in all.

Power, as the saying is, no doubt put the man to the test. It brought new temptations and therefore new failures, from which the shepherd of the desert might have remained free. But happy is the man who, living

> " In the fierce light that beats upon a throne,
>   And blackens every blot,"

can stand the test as well as did Mohammed. A Christian poet has well asked—

> "What keeps a spirit wholly true
>   To that ideal which he bears?
>   What record? not the sinless years
> That breathed beneath the Syrian blue."

But it is a current misconception, and, subject to the above explanation, a very great one, that a gradual but continuous and accelerating moral declension is to be traced from the time when the fugitive unexpectedly entered Medina in triumph. "Truth is come—let falsehood disappear," he said, when, after his long exile, and

after the temptations of Medina had done their worst
for him, he re-entered the Kaaba, and its three hundred
and sixty idols, the famous Hobal among them, vanished before him ; and in his treatment of the unbeliev-
ing city he was marvelously true to his programme.
There was now nothing left in Mecca that could thwart
his pleasure. If ever he had worn a mask at all, he
would now at all events have thrown it off; if lower
aims had gradually sapped the higher, or his moderation had been directed, as Gibbon supposes, by his selfish interests, we should now have seen the effect; now
would have been the moment to gratify his ambition,
to satiate his lust, to glut his revenge. Is there any
thing of the kind ? Read the account of the entry of
Mohammed into Mecca, side by side with that of Ma-
rius or Sulla into Rome. Compare all the attendant
circumstances, the outrages that preceded, and the use
made by each of his recovered power, and we shall
then be in a position better to appreciate the magnanimity and moderation of the Prophet of Arabia. There
were no proscription lists, no plunder, no wanton revenge.

The chief blots in his fame are not after his undisputed victory, but during his years of checkered warfare at
Medina, and, such as they are, are distributed very even-
ly over the whole of that time. In other words, he did

very occasionally give way to a strong temptation; but there was no gradual sapping of moral principles and no deadening of conscience—a very important distinction. One or two acts of summary and uncompromising punishment; possibly one or two acts of cunning, and, after Kadijah was dead, the violation of one law which he had from veneration for her imposed on others, and had always hitherto kept himself, form no very long bill of indictment against one who always admitted he was a man of like passions with ourselves, who was ignorant of the Christian moral law, and who attained to power after difficulties and dangers and misconceptions which might have turned the best of men into a suspicious and sanguinary tyrant.*

It is no doubt true that some of the revelations of the Koran, particularly the later ones, bear the appearance of having been given consciously for personal and temporary purposes, and these have led, with some show of reason, even such impartial writers as Sir William Muir to accuse Mohammed of " the high blasphemy of forging the name of God." But it would be strange indeed

---

* Yet Sprenger (vol. i., p. 359), on no more grounds than those here mentioned, can say of Mohammed that when he attained to power in Medina, "er wurde zum wollüstigen Theokraten und blutdürstig Tyrannen, Pabst und König." What Christian Pope or King—to say nothing of Oriental rulers, with whom alone is it fair to compare him—had as great temptations and succumbed to them as little as did Mohammed?

if, viewed in the light of what I have said above as to Mohammed's unfaltering belief in his own inspiration, he had not occasionally, or even often, revealed in the Koran the mental processes by which he justified to himself acts about which he may have himself, at first, felt scruples, or which his contemporaries may have called in question. And it seems pertinent to ask, by way of rebutting the charge, whether he was not at least equally ready, when occasion required, to blame himself for what he had said or done, and to call the whole Mussulman world to be witnesses of his self-condemnation? And, again, if he was ever, in the matter of the Koran, a conscious impostor, why was he not so much oftener? If he had once knowingly tripped, and gained thereby, the path must have been too slippery and the descent must have seemed too easy and inviting for him to recall his footsteps. But what are the facts? Take two samples.

On one occasion, in a moment of despondency, he made a partial concession to idolatry. He thought to win over the recalcitrant Koreishites to his views by allowing that their gods might make intercession with the supreme God.

"What think ye of Al-Lat, and Al-Uzza, and Manah, the third besides? They are the exalted Females, and their intercession with God may be hoped for."

The Koreishites, overjoyed, signified their adhesion to

Mohammed, and it seemed that they would bring over all Mecca with them. His friends would have passed the matter over as quietly as possible. So great was the scandal among the Faithful that some of his earliest historians omit it altogether. But the Prophet's conscience was too tender for that. In an hour of weakness Mohammed had mistaken expediency for duty, and having discovered his mistake, he would recall the concession, at all hazards, as publicly as he had made it, even at the risk of the imputation of weakness and of imposture. The amended version of the Sura ran thus:

"What think ye of Al-Lat, and Al-Uzza, and Manah, the third besides? They are naught but empty names which ye and your fathers have invented."*

I will give one more instance. It is a memorable one. Mohammed was engaged in earnest conversation with Wallid, a powerful Koreishite, whose conversion he much desired. A blind man in very humble circumstances, Abdallah by name, happened to come up, and, not knowing that Mohammed was otherwise engaged, exclaimed, "Oh, Apostle of God, teach me some part of what God has taught thee." Mohammed, vexed at the interruption, frowned and turned away from him. But

* Sura liii.; cf. also xvii., 75, and xxii., 51; see Muir, vol. ii., p. 149–158, and Sprenger, vol. ii., p. 17, where there is a curious dissertation on the word Gharânyk, used for Females—" swans which mount higher and higher toward God."

his conscience soon smote him for having postponed the poor and humble to the rich and powerful, and the next day's Sura showed that this "forger of God's name" was at least as ready to forge it for his own condemnation as in his defense. The Sura is known by the significant title "He frowned," and runs thus:

"The Prophet frowned, and turned aside,
　Because the blind man came unto him.
And how knowest thou whether he might not have been cleansed from
　　his sins,
Or whether he might have been admonished, and profited thereby?
　As for the man that is rich,
　Him thou receivest graciously;
And thou carest not that he is not cleansed.
But as for him that cometh unto thee earnestly seeking his salvation,
And trembling anxiously, him dost thou neglect.
　By no means shouldst thou act thus."

And ever after this we are told that, when the Prophet saw the poor blind man, he went out of his way to do him honor, saying, "The man is thrice welcome on whose account my Lord hath reprimanded me," and he made him twice Governor of Medina.*

Mohammed never wavered in his belief in his own

---

* Sura lxxx., with Sale's note ad loc.; and Muir, vol. ii., p. 128. Sir Wm. Muir tells the story much as I have related it, but seems quite unable to see its grandeur, for he only remarks upon it: "This incident illustrates at once the anxiety of Mohammed to gain over the principal men of the Koreish, and, when he was rejected, the readiness with which he turned to the poor and uninfluential." Was ever moral sublimity so marred, or heroism so vulgarized? How Mohammed towers above even his best historians!

mission, nor, what is more extraordinary, in his belief as
to its precise nature and well-defined limits. He was a
prophet charged with a mission from God; nothing less,
but nothing more. He might make mistakes, lose battles, do wrong acts, but none the less did he believe that
the words he spoke were the very words of God. To
every Sura of the Koran he prefixed the words, "In the
name of God, the Compassionate, the Merciful," even as
the Hebrew prophet would open his message with his
"Thus saith the Lord;" and before every sentence and
every word of the Sacred Book is to be read, between
the lines, the word "say," indicating that Mohammed
believed, what Moses and Isaiah only believed on special
occasions, that in his utterances he was the mere mouthpiece, and therefore the unerring mouthpiece, of the Infinite and the Eternal. He might win his way against
superhuman difficulties, preserve a charmed life, do deeds
which seemed miracles to others, gain the homage of all
Arabia, and present in his own person an ideal of morality never before pictured by an Arab; and yet he never
forgot himself, or claimed to be more than a weak and
fallible mortal.

As his view of his own mission is an all-important
point in estimating his character, let us deal, in concluding this Lecture, with facts alone, and watch his conduct
at a few critical epochs which I have purposely selected,

as throwing light upon the matter, in its different aspects, away from their chronological order and from very different periods of his life.

When the Persian monarch Chosroes was contemplating with pride, like Nebuchadnezzar of old, the great Artemita that he had built and all its fabulous treasures, he received a letter from an obscure citizen of Mecca, bidding him acknowledge Mohammed as the Prophet of God. Chosroes tore the letter into pieces. "It is thus," exclaimed the Arabian Prophet when he heard of it, "that God will tear his kingdom and reject his supplications." No prediction could have seemed at the time less likely to be accomplished, since Persia was at its height, and Constantinople at its lowest. But Mohammed lived to see its fulfillment, and yet never claimed in consequence, as others might have done, the power of prophecy.

While he had as yet only half established his position, a powerful Christian tribe tendered their submission, if only he would leave their chief some remnant of his power. "Not one unripe date," replied Mohammed.* We remember how the French rhetorician the other day, knowing that his nation, if they are slaves to nothing else, are always slaves to an epigram, prolonged re-

---

* Muir, vol. iv., p. 59.

sistance to the bitter end by his famous declaration that not " an inch of their territory nor a stone of their fortresses" would the French surrender.   And we may imagine the effect produced upon the handful of Mohammed's Meccan followers who were still in exile at Medina by such an answer, coming from one who was certainly no vapid rhetorician, who preferred silence to speech, and who never said a thing he did not really mean.

Moseilama, the most formidable of the rival prophets whom Mohammed's success stirred up, thinking that Mohammed's game was a merely selfish one, and that two might play at it, sent to Mohammed to offer to go shares with him in the good things of the world, which united they might easily divide.   The letter was of Spartan brevity: " Moseilama the apostle of God to Mohammed the apostle of God.—Now let the earth be half mine and half thine."   Mohammed's reply was hardly less laconic: " Mohammed the apostle of God to Moseilama the liar.—The earth is God's; he giveth it to such of his servants as he pleaseth, and they who fear him shall prosper."

Again mark his conduct under failure or rebuff.   He had lost, within three days of each other, Abu Taleb, his one protector, and his venerable wife Kadijah—that toothless old woman, as Ayesha long afterward, in the bloom of her beauty, called her; the wife who, as Mohammed indignantly replied, "when he was poor, had enriched him; when he was called a liar, had alone believed in him; when he was opposed by all the world, had alone remained true to him."* What was he to do? Silence and the desert seemed the one chance of safety, but what did he do? Followed only by Zeid, his faithful freedman, he went to Tayif, the town after Mecca most wholly given to idolatry; and, like Elijah in Samaria, he boldly challenged the protection and obedience of the inhabitants. They stoned him out of the city. He returned to Mecca defeated, but not disheartened; cast down, but not destroyed; quietly saying to himself, "If thou, O Lord, art not angry, I am safe; I seek refuge in the light of thy countenance alone."†

After the tide had turned in his favor, and the battle of Bedr had, as it seemed, put the seal to his military success, he was signally defeated and wounded almost

---

* Sprenger characteristically remarks (vol. i., p. 151) that Mohammed's faithfulness to Kadijah to her dying day was due probably not to his inclination, but to his dependence on her. Why, then, the interval before Mohammed married again? And why, long afterward, his noble burst of gratitude to her memory when Ayesha contrasted her own youth and beauty with Kadijah's age and infirmities, and asked, "Am not I much better than she?" "No, by Allah," replied Mohammed—"No, by Allah; when I was poor she enriched me," etc. Was Mohammed dependent upon the dead? For cynical remarks of a similar kind, see, among many other instances, Sprenger, vol. ii., p. 19, 23, 86.

† See the story in full in Muir, vol. ii., p. 198–203.

to the death at Mount Ohud. People began to desert him; but a Sura, Mohammed's " order of the day," appeared: " Mohammed is no more than a prophet. What if he had been killed, needs ye go back? He that turneth back injureth not God in the least, but himself."* The spell of his untaught eloquence recalled them to themselves, and we are assured that his defeat at Ohud advanced his cause as much as did his victory at Bedr.

Ayesha, his favorite wife, one day asked of him, " Oh, Prophet of God, do none enter Paradise but through God's mercy?" "None, none, none," replied he. "But will not even you enter by your own merits?" Mohammed put his hand upon his head and thrice replied, " Neither shall I enter Paradise unless God cover me with his mercy." There was no " false certitude of the divine intentions," the besetting temptation of spiritual ambition; no facile dogmatizing upon what he had only to hint to be believed—his own pre-eminent position in the unseen world. It would have been safe to do so: ἐς ἀφανὲς τὸν μῦθον ἀνενείκας οὐκ ἔχει ἔλεγχον;† and how few could have resisted a like temptation!

And at the last grand scene of all, when the Prophet had met his death, as he had always told his doubting followers he must, and Omar, the Simon Peter of Islam,

---

* Sura iii., 138.
† Hdt., ii., 23.

in the agony of his grief, drew his scimiter and, wildly rushing in among the weeping Mussulmans, swore that he would strike off the head of any one who dared to say that the Prophet was dead—the Prophet could not be dead—it was by a gentle reminder of what the Prophet himself had always taught that the venerable Abu Bakr, the earliest of the Prophet's friends, and his successor in the Kaliphate, calmed his excitement: " Is it then Mohammed, or the God of Mohammed, that we have learned to worship ?"

# LECTURE III.

FEBRUARY 28, 1874.

## MOHAMMEDANISM.

" Allahu Akbar "—God is great; there is no god but God, and Mohammed is his prophet.

In the concluding part of my last Lecture I discussed
at length the question of the character of Mohammed,
and we arrived, I think, at the conclusion that, on the
one hand, he had grave moral faults, which may be accounted for, but not excused, by the circumstances of
time, by the exigencies of his situation, and by the weaknesses of human nature.  And on the other we saw reason to believe that he was not only passionately impress-
ed with the reality of his divine mission in early life,
but that the common view of a great moral declension
to be traced in his latter years is not borne out by
the evidence; and that to the end of his career, amid
failures and successes, in life and in preparation for
death, he was true to the one principle with which he
started.  He became indeed, by the force of circum-

stances, general and ruler, lawgiver and judge, of all Arabia; but above all and before all, he was still a simple prophet delivering God's message in singleness of heart, obeying, as far as he could, God's will, but never claiming to be more than God's weak and erring servant.

And now, perhaps, it is time to ask what was the essence of Mohammed's belief, that which made him what he was, which has given his religion its inexhaustible vitality? How did it resemble, and how did it differ from, the religions which it overthrew, and one of which at least we are accustomed to look upon, and shall, in its pure form as it came from Christ's own lips, and can still be read in Christ's own acts, and even to some extent in the character of his servants, always continue to look upon, as immeasurably superior to Mohammedanism?

The essence of Mohammedanism is not merely the sublime belief in the unity of God, though it is difficult for us to realize the tumult of the feelings and the intensity of the life which must be awakened in a Polytheistic people, who are also imaginative and energetic, when, on a sudden, they recognize the One in and behind the Many. Mohammed started indeed with the dogmatic assertion that there was but one God, the Creator of all things in heaven and earth, all powerful, knowing all things, every where present. He reiterates this in a thousand shapes as the forefront of his message ;* and, sublimely confident that it need only be stated to insure ultimate acceptance, he deigns not to offer proof of that which, in his judgment, must prove itself.

But it was more than the unity of God, and the attributes which flow from that conception, which Mohammed asserted. A theoretic assent to this might have had but little influence on practice. What is by its nature immeasurably above man may also be immeasurably removed from him ; and accordingly Mohammed reasserted that which had been the life of the old Hebrew nation, and the burden of the song of every Hebrew prophet— that God not only lives, but that he is a righteous and a merciful ruler ; and that to his will it is the duty and the privilege of all living men to bow.† Nor was the sublimity of this doctrine marred in its application by the old Hebrew exclusiveness. The Arabian nation was first

---

* See especially Suras i. and cxii., the beginning and end of the Koran in the orthodox arrangement ; also Sura xxxv., 41–44. Cf. also Sura ii., 19–20, 109 ; vi., 1–6 ; xiii., 10, 11 ; xvi., 12–17 ; liii. and xcvi.

† See this well drawn out in Maurice's "Religions of the World," p. 21–24. The passage is a most suggestive one. I owe much to it; and it seems to me that here, and in many other passages of his writings, Mr. Maurice did far more, and penetrated far deeper, than is allowed in a very brilliant passage of a recent work (see "Literature and Dogma," p. 345). When the unacknowledged debts of the nineteenth century to its great writers come to be added up, I am convinced that it will be fully recognized that the mental powers of Mr. Maurice rank as high as did the purity and nobility of his life ; and more can hardly be said.

called indeed; but as in Christianity, and as it was not in Judaism, the obligations of the Arabs were to be measured by their privileges, and the call was to be extended through them to the world at large. The Jew surrendered his birthright if he imparted his faith to other peoples. The Arab surrendered his if he did not spread his faith wherever and however he could.

But Mohammed's assertion of the unity of God, and of his rule over every detail of man's life, was no mere plagiarism from an older faith. The Jewish people at large had, even in their best days, rushed wildly after the worship of alien gods; at last, indeed, the iron of the Captivity had entered into their souls; they learned much during their sojourn in the East, but they unlearned more —they unlearned there, once and forever, the sin of idolatry. But though they never henceforward worshiped other gods, the higher teaching of their prophets they still too much ignored, and the period which might have been the culmination of their glory ended in that tragedy of tragedies which was the immediate precursor of their fall. The sceptre departed from Judah, but the Jewish exiles in Arabia still clung desperately to the phantom of those proud religious privileges when all which had given some claim to them had disappeared. Christians too—such Christians as Mohammed had ever met—had forgotten at once the faith of the Jews, and that higher revelation of God given to them by Christ which the Jews rejected. Homoousians and Homoiousians, Monothelites and Monophysites, Jacobites and Eutychians, making hard dogmas of things wherein the sacred writers themselves had made no dogma, disputing fiercely whether what was mathematically false could be metaphysically true, and nicely discriminating the shades of truth and falsehood in the views suggested to bridge over the abysmal gulf between them; turning figures into facts, rhetoric into logic, and poetry into prose, had forgotten the unity of God while they were disputing about it most loudly with their lips. They busied themselves with every question about Christ except those which might have led them to imitate Christ's life. Now Mohammed came to make a clean sweep of such unrealities. Images : what are they ?  " Bits of black wood, pretending to be God ;"* philosophical theories, and theological cobwebs. Away with them all ! God is great, and there is nothing else great. This is the Mussulman creed. "Islam," that is, man must resign his will to God's, and find his highest happiness in so doing. This is the Mussulman life. And I would remark here, and would particularly beg those who are doing me the honor to attend these Lectures to bear in mind, that though I have, in

---

* Carlyle, " Heroes," p. 226.

compliance with European custom, often spoken of Mohammedanism and Mohammedans, the name was never
used by Mohammed himself or by his earlier disciples,
and, in spite of the reverence paid to their Prophet, it
has always been rejected by his followers themselves as
a rightful appellation. To quote once more the noble
words of Abu Bakr, it was not Mohammed, but the God
of Mohammed, that the Prophet taught his followers to
worship. The creed is "Islam," a verbal noun, derived
from a root meaning "submission to" and "faith in God,"
and the believers who so submit themselves are called
Moslems, a participle of the same root, both being connected with the words "Salam," or "peace," and "Sa-
lym," or "healthy."* There was nothing, therefore, theoretically new in what I have described as the central
truth of Islam, for it was this belief that lay at the root of
the greatness of the Jewish nation, and their separation
from all other nations. Certain forms of Christianity
have asserted it as strongly as did Mohammed. This
principle has been the strength of Calvinism and of Pu-
ritanism; and in this direction perhaps lies the explanation of the fact that those forms of religion which have
been theoretically most fatalistic have by their acts given
the strongest practical assertion of free-will. This was

---

* Sprenger, vol. i., p. 69.

the spark from heaven which lit the train. In his assertion of this lay the religious genius of Mohammed. This gave the Arabs " unity as a nation, discipline and enthusiasm as an army."* This sent them forth in their wild crusade against the world; and, armed with this, they swept away before them every creed, or memory of a creed, which did not then contain any principle so inspiring.

Such then were the two leading principles of the new creed: the existence of one God, whose will was to be the rule of life, and the mission of Mohammed to proclaim what that will was. The one doctrine as old, if not older than the time when the father of the faithful left his Chaldean home in obedience to the divine will; the other sanctioned, indeed, in its general assertion of the prophetic office, by the traditionary belief of both Jews and Arabs; but startling enough in the time at which the revelation came, in the instrument selected, and in the way in which he proclaimed it. In this consists the real originality, such as it is, of Mohammedanism. The other articles of faith, added to the two I have already discussed—the written revelation of God's will, the responsibility of man, the existence of angels and of Jinn, the future life, the resurrection, and the final judg-

---

* Maurice, loc. cit.

ment—are to be found, either developed or in germ, in the systems either of Jews or Zoroastrians or Christians. Even in the times of ignorance, the camel tethered to a dead man's grave was an indication that the grave was, even to the wild Arab, not the end of all things.*

Nor was there any thing much more original in the four practical duties of Islam—in prayer and almsgiving, in fasting and in pilgrimage.† Prayer is the aspiration of the human soul toward God, common to every relig- ion, from the rudest Fetichism to the most sublime Mono- theism. Almsgiving is the most easy and obvious meth- od of evidencing that love to man which leads up to and is, in its turn, the result of love to God. Fasting is an assertion, though a superficial one, of the great truth that self-denial is a step toward God ; but it is peculiarly li- able to abuse as fostering the belief, so common among the ruder of the Semitic nations, and still commoner among ascetics in modern times, that God is to be feared rather than loved, and that there is something pleasing

---

* Sprenger says (vol. i., p. 4, 301) that the reason why Mohammed re- fers so often, *e. g.*, in the very first Sura in chronological order, to the "clot of blood" from which man was created, is because he looked upon it much as Christians have done to the emerging of the butterfly from the chrysalis as a proof or illustration of the resurrection. In Sura liii. Mohammed says he took not the doctrine merely, but the illustration also, from the roll of Abraham. Cf. Sura lxxv., entitled "The Resurrection," ad fin.: "Is not the God who formed man from a mere embryo powerful enough to quicken the dead?"

† Cf. Milman, "Latin Christianity," vol. i., p. 453.

to him in pain as such—pain, that is, apart from its effect upon the will, and so upon the character.    Pilgrimage is a concession to human feelings, not to say to human weakness, common again, in practice, to all the religions of the world.    But this last calls, perhaps, for some special remark here, since its actual influence has been so great, while in theory and in reality it is alien alike to Mohammedanism and to Christianity.

"The hour cometh when ye shall neither in this mountain nor yet in Jerusalem worship the Father."   "God is a spirit, and they that worship him must worship him in spirit and in truth."   But from the time the words were spoken, even to this day, a continuous living stream has poured toward the Holy Land.   For nineteen centuries Christian pilgrims have been seen to leave their homes and kindred, facing, now privations, now dangers, and now ridicule, that they might enjoy the sacred luxury, the ineffable religious rapture, of beholding the city over which the Saviour wept, of standing on the spot which gave him birth, of gazing on the lake whereon he taught, and of worshiping in the shrine which covers the rock wherein his body lay.    And far be it from me to say—spite of the invention of the true cross, spite of St. Andrew's lance and the relics of the Apostles, spite of the Crusades themselves, spite of the keys of the Holy Sepulchre, and even of the imposture of the holy fire—

that the evils belonging to this reverence for places have altogether predominated over the good. A scientific and unimaginative age laughs at the weaknesses and the follies involved, but it forgets the dauntless faith and heroic endurance, the sacrifice of self, and the romance of danger; it forgets that it is the office of religion to deal with these very human weaknesses and follies, and make the best of such materials as it has to work upon.

Christ swept away some of the abuses of the Temple worship, and looked forward to its ultimate abolition; but he did not sweep away the Temple itself. He rather paid it its customary honors. Mohammed saw the dangers of the Kaaba worship, and, once and again, proposed to destroy it altogether; but he had to deal with an historical faith, and with a shrine of immemorial antiquity, one which Diodorus Siculus, a hundred years before the Christian era, tells us was even then "most ancient, and was exceedingly revered by the whole Arab race." The traditions of the Kaaba ran back to Ishmael and Abraham—nay, even to Seth and Adam;* and, as its very name, "Beit Allah," shows, it

---

* Cf. Sura iii., 90. "The first temple that was founded for mankind was that in Becca (place of resort, *i. e.*, Mecca)—Blessed, and a guidance to human beings. In it are evident signs, even the standing-place of Abraham, and he who entereth it is safe. And the pilgrimage to the temple is a service due to God from those who are able to journey thither." This sentence is still woven into the covering of the Kaaba sent annually by the Sultan.

might, in its first rude shape, have been erected by
some such ancient patriarch as he who raised a pillar
of rough stone where in his sleep he had seen the
angels ascending and descending, and called it "Bethel,
or Beit Allah: this is the house of God, and this the
gate of heaven." Mohammed cherished also all the
family associations of a Haschimite,* and all the local
affections of a Meccan patriot; and the family, and the
place, and the country, the historical lore and the religious imagination, combined to save the sacred shrine.
Mohammed swept away the idols of the Kaaba; he
abolished the nude processions† and the other abuses
of its worship, but he retained the Kaaba itself; and
the quaint rites, which were old in Mohammed's time,
are still religiously observed by the whole Mohammedan world. Seven times the pilgrim walks around
the sacred mosque, seven times he kisses the Black
Stone; he drinks the brackish water of the sacred
well Zemzem, buries the parings of his nails and the
hair he has at length shaved in the consecrated
ground; he ascends Mount Arafat, and showers stones
on the three mysterious pillars.‡ Nor is the Kaaba

* See a curious conversation between Mohammed and Ayesha on the
Kaaba, illustrating the strong family feelings of the Prophet. Sprenger,
vol. i., p. 315.

† Sura vii., 27, seq.  Cf. xxii., 27–40.

‡ A plan of the Kaaba, as taken by Ali Bey, and a full description of

present to the mind at those times only when the prescribed pilgrimage is near at hand, in prospect or in retrospect. The first architectural requisite of every Mussulman house is the niche or arch which points with mathematical precision to the sacred pile; and, guided by this, every devout Mussulman turns five times a day toward the Kiblah of the world in earnest prayer to God. "That man," says Dr. Johnson, "has little to be envied whose patriotism would not gain force on the plains of Marathon, or whose piety would not grow warm among the ruins of Iona." The ceremonies of the Kaaba may perhaps seem to us ridiculous, but the shrine is one which kindled the feelings of the Arab patriot, and roused the hopes of the Bedouin of the desert, ages before Miltiades fought, and tens of ages before Columban preached. It has been consecrated in its later history by its connection with the grandest forward movement that the Eastern world has ever known; and, in spite of the mummeries and the abuses which have grown around the pilgrimage of the Hadj in the course of ages, I should be slow indeed to assert that the feelings which still draw, year

---

the pilgrim ceremonies, which he himself went through, may be seen in Burton's "Pilgrimage," vol. iii., p. 61. Burckhardt and Burton have both described the Black Stone minutely from personal observation; and a picture of it, the size of the original, is given in Muir, vol. ii., p. 18.

after year, Mussulmans by myriads from the burning sands of Africa, from the snows of Siberia, and the coral reefs of the Malays, toward a barren valley in Arabia, do not, on the whole, elevate rather than depress them in the scale of humanity.  In their own rough and imperfect way, they raise the mind of the nomad and the shepherd from the animal life of the present to the memories of the distant past, and the hopes of the far future.  They are a living testimony to the unity of God, and a homage paid by the world to that Prophet who softened the savage breast and elevated the savage mind, and taught them what, but for him, they had never learned at all.

It will be apparent, from what I have already said, that of the previous faiths existing in the world, the one which influenced Mohammed most was, beyond all question, Judaism.  Insomuch that one who probably, with the single exception of Dr. Sprenger, knew more of the literature of the two faiths than any living man —one whose loss all who take interest in Eastern ques- tions are now deploring, and one who, had he lived, would probably have done ampler justice to Islam and its founder than perhaps any one else has done or can do—the late Emanuel Deutsch, summed up the con- nection between them in the celebrated dictum, that " when the Talmud was gathered in, the Koran began

—*post hoc ergo propter hoc.*" And he went on to indorse and to develop what Dean Milman had hinted before him, that Islam was little else than a republication
of Judaism, with such modifications as suited it to Arabian soil, *plus* the important addition of the prophetic
mission of Mohammed.* The gifted author was, perhaps, from the very extent of his knowledge of Tal-
mudical literature, prone to trace its influence every
where; and the proposition is, perhaps, stated a little
too nakedly, and, as he, no doubt, would have been
the first to admit, needs some important qualifications;
but nobody would deny that it is substantially true.
Indeed, the general connection between race and creed
has been proved by the Science of Comparative Religion to be so intimate, that it could hardly in any
case have been otherwise. It seems a cruel destiny
that allows a man of great original genius to accumu-
late such vast stores of recondite learning, and then
snatches him away before he has had time to do more
than leave the world dimly and sadly conscious of
what it has lost in losing him!

Anyhow, the Koran teems with ideas, allusions, and

---

* It must be remembered also that the ceremonialism of the Jews for
the time almost entirely disappeared. For a full account of the influence
of the Essenic communities and their doctrines on the rise of Islam, see
Sprenger, vol. i., p. 17–21, and p. 30–35; and for that of the Ebionites
or Judaizing Christians to the east of the Jordan, p. 21–28.

even phraseology, drawn not so much from the written as from the oral Jewish law, from the traditions that grew around it, and the commentaries on it. The Talmud, in its two divisions of Halacha and Haggada, sums up the intellectual and social and religious life of the Jews during a period of nearly a thousand years. It is the meeting-point of the three Monotheistic creeds of the world; and, even with the imperfect information that Eastern scholars have yet given respecting it, it has done much to throw light upon them all. Mohammed was never backward to acknowledge the intimate connection between his faith and that of the Jews. And in more than one passage of the Koran he refers with equal respect to their oral and to their written law. Nor did Christ really draw so broad a distinction between these two as might be imagined from the sweeping way in which he sometimes denounces the Scribes and Pharisees. "Whatsoever they that sit in Moses's seat bid you observe, that observe and do."[*] And it is incontestable that the Pharisees, as a body, contained some of the best and noblest—Hillel and Shammai, Gamaliel and St. Paul—as it contained some of the worst and meanest, of their nation.

---

[*] St. Matt. xxiii., 2–3. See this well argued in an article on the Talmud, *Edinburgh Review* for July, 1873.

And, accordingly, Mohammed, during the early years of the Hegira, struggled hard, and, as it might have seemed to him, with every prospect of success, to secure the adhesion of the Jewish tribes who dwelt around Medina. He appealed to their Scriptures, which, he said, he came not to destroy, but to fulfill, and which, as he argued, for those who had eyes to see, pointed to him. " A prophet shall the Lord your God raise up unto you of your brethren like unto me ; to him shall ye hearken." " Was he not like unto Moses ?" he asked again and again ; " and did he not spring from their brethren, the children of Ishmael ?" He adapted the fasts and the feasts of the new religion to their model. He took from them the law of usury and the law of inheritance. He owes to them some of his regulations respecting ablutions and unclean animals. He even, till he could hope no longer, made Jerusalem the Kiblah of the world for the five daily prayers.

It must have surprised Mohammed, with his half-knowledge of their history, that the Jews should be unable to enter into his views of a great catholic creed, or Religion of Humanity—the creed of Abraham—embracing Jews, Arabs, and Christians in one body. But it can surprise no one who has ever in any degree entered into the religious genius of the Jewish race, or who has reflected on the almost insuperable difficulties

which lay in the way of the Jews accepting that higher creed, the Author of which it is their eternal honor
to have produced, and their tragic destiny to have
rejected.   And the Bani Kainucaa, and the Bani Na-
dhir, the Bani Koreitsa, and the Jews of Kheibar, bit-
terly experienced in Mohammed's subsequent treatment
of them the truth of the now all-too-familiar maxim
in ecclesiastical history that they who differ least in
religious matters hate the most.

It is impossible to gain for one's self, and almost equally so to give to others within a short space of time, any
thing like an adequate idea either of the form or of the
contents of the book of which Mohammed, whatever
the general influences brought to bear upon his mind,
was the undisputed author, and which still underlies
the life of the vast fabric of the Mohammedan world.
In my first Lecture I compared and contrasted the
Koran with the Bible; but it is necessary, perhaps, to
say something more of its leading characteristics, or the
want of them.   The Koran defies analysis, for that pre-
supposes something like method in the thing to be ana-
lyzed.   It can hardly be characterized by any one epi-
thet, for there is not a single Sura of any length which
sustains a uniform character throughout.   It has often
been remarked that there is no more striking proof of
the discrepancies of national taste than the diametrical-

ly opposite opinions held by the cultivated classes of East and West on the literary merits of the Koran. Having performed repeatedly, for the purpose of these Lectures, a task which Bunsen and Sprenger and Renan all pronounce to be almost impossible—that of reading the Koran continuously from beginning to end, both in the orthodox and chronological order—I have acquired a better right, perhaps, than most people to indorse the superficial opinion that dullness is, to a European who is ignorant of Arabic, the prevailing characteristic of the book as a whole until he begins to make a minute study of it. The importance of the subjects it handles, the unique interest attaching to the speaker, and the unaffected reverence with which every utterance is still regarded by so large a portion of the world, are insufficient to redeem it from this general reproach.

Endless assertions as to what the Koran is, and what it is not, warnings drawn from previous Arabian history, especially the lost tribes of Ad and Thamud; Jewish or Arab legends of the heroes of the Old Testament—stories told, and, it must be added, often spoiled in the telling of them; laws, ceremonial and moral, civil and sumptuary; personal apologies; curses showered upon Abu Lahab or the whole community of the Jews; all this alternates with sublime revelations of the attributes of the Godhead, bursts of admiration for Christ him-self—though not for the views held of him by his so-called followers—flights of poetry, scathing rebukes of the hypocrite, the ungrateful, the unmerciful.

That the book as a whole is a medley, however it may be arranged, will seem only natural when we re-member the way in which it was composed, preserved, edited, and stereotyped. Dictated from time to time by Mohammed to his disciples, it was by them partly treasured in their memories, partly written down on shoulder-bones of mutton or on oyster shells, on bits of wood or tablets of stone, which, being thrown pell-mell into boxes, and jumbled up together, like the leaves of the Cumean Sibyl after a gust of wind, were not put into any shape at all till after the Prophet's death by order of Abu Bakr. The work of the editor consisted simply in arranging the Suras in the order of their re-spective lengths—the longest first, the shortest last; and, though the book once afterward passed through the ed-itor's hands, this is substantially the shape in which the Koran has come down to us. Various readings, which would seem, however, to have been of very slight im-portance, having crept into the different copies, a re-vising committee was appointed by order of the Kaliph Othman, and an authorized edition having been thus prepared "to prevent the texts differing, like those of the

Jews and Christians," all previous copies were collected and burned.

Nor is it to be wondered at that the principle of arrangement, combined with the impossibility of keeping the rhyme or rhythm in any translation, have prevented European critics, as a body, from indorsing the judgment, not merely of Mohammed himself, for that, if it had stood alone, might be looked upon as partial, but also of the whole Eastern world.

"If ye be in doubt as to our revelation to our servant, then produce a Sura like unto it, and summon your witnesses, God and all, if ye be men of truth."*

And again, "If men and genii were assembled together that they might produce a book like the Koran, they must fail."†

It is to be remarked that Mohammed and Mohammed's enemies are quite at one as to the merits of the book. The Arabs said that the Koran could not be Mohammed's work because it was too good. Mohammed replied to the effect that they were both right and wrong. They were right, for it was too good for Mohammed uninspired; they were wrong, for it was too good to have come originally from any one but the All-Merciful.‡

---

* Sura ii., 21.                                              † Sura xvii., 90.
‡ Sura xvi., 105, compared with xxv., 5, etc.

Of course, by the existing arrangement, even such psychological development as there was in the Koran has been obscured; for, as a rule, what the editor put last comes really first.  These are the burning utterances of the Prophet, who knows no influence but the inspiration pent within him; in these are the pith and poetry of the whole; while the elaborate and labored arguments, the *apologiæ pro vitâ suâ*, are the product of the mind which the force of circumstances and the love of spiritual power—that most exquisite and most dangerous of fascinations—had driven to become conscious of itself.  The very titles of the earlier Suras, the imprecations with which they abound, the imagery they employ, suggest the shepherd of the desert, the despised visionary, the poet and the prophet.  " The folding up," "the cleaving in sunder," "the celestial signs," "the unity," "the overwhelming," "the striking," "the inevitable," "the earthquake," "the war-horses," tell their own story.  There are passages in these, though it must be admitted they are rare, which may be compared in grandeur even with some of the sublimest passages of Job, of David, or of Isaiah.

Take, for instance, the vision of the last day with which the eighty-first Sura, " The folding up," begins:

" When the sun shall be folded up,
    And when the stars shall fall,
    And when the mountains shall be set in motion,

And when the she-camels with young shall be neglected,
And when the wild beasts shall be huddled together,
And when the seas shall boil,
And when souls shall be joined again to their bodies,
And when the female child that had been buried alive shall ask for
    what crime she was put to death,
And when the leaves of the Book shall be unrolled,
And when the Heavens shall be stripped away like a skin,
And when Hell shall be made to blaze,
And when Paradise shall be brought near—
Every soul shall know what it has done."

Allusions to the monotony of the desert; the sun in its rising brightness; the moon in its splendor; are varied in the Koran by much more vivid mental visions of the Great Day when men shall be like moths scattered abroad, and the mountains shall become like carded wool of various colors, driven by the wind. No wonder that Labyd, the greatest poet of his time, forbore to enter the poetic lists with Mohammed when he recited to him the description of the infidel in the second Sura:

"They are like one who kindleth a fire, and when it hath thrown its light on all around him, God taketh away the light and leaveth him in darkness, and they can not see."

"Deaf, dumb, blind, therefore they shall not retrace their steps."

"They are like those who, when there cometh a storm-cloud out of heaven big with darkness, thunder, and lightning, thrust their fingers into their ears because of the thunder-clap for fear of death. God is round about the infidels."

"The lightning almost snatcheth away their eyes: so oft as it gleameth on them, they walk on in it; but when darkness closeth upon them, they stop; and if God pleased, of their ears and of their eyes would he surely deprive them: verily God is almighty."

And at the end of the same Sura, which, it is to be remembered, appeared quite late in the Prophet's life, at a period when it might have been expected that the cares of government would dim the brightness of the Prophet's visions, we find the sublime description of Him whom it had been the mission of his life to proclaim, and which is still engraved on precious stones, and worn by devout Mussulmans:

"God! there is no god but he, the Living, the Eternal. Slumber doth not overtake him, neither sleep; to him belongeth all that is in heaven and in earth. Who is he that can intercede with him but by his own permission? He knoweth that which is past and that which is to come unto them, and they shall not comprehend any thing of his knowledge but so far as he pleaseth. His throne is extended over heaven and earth, and the upholding of both is no burden unto him. He is the Lofty and the Great."

Almost equally well too, as a proof of his poetic

inspiration, Mohammed might have quoted that other description of Infidelity, also produced late in his life, and pronounced by Sir William Muir and by Emanuel Deutsch to be one of the grandest in the whole Koran:

"As to the infidels, their works are like the Serab on the plain,\* which the thirsty traveler thinketh to be water, and then, when he cometh thereto, he findeth it to be nothing; but he findeth God about him, and he will fully pay him his account; for swift in taking an account is God;

"Or as the darkness over a deep sea, billows riding upon billows below, and clouds above; one darkness on another darkness: when a man stretcheth forth his hand he is far from seeing it; he to whom God doth not grant light, no light at all hath he." †

Strange and graphic accounts have been preserved to us by Ayesha of the physical phenomena attending the Prophet's fits of inspiration. He heard as it were the ringing of a bell; he fell down as one dead; he sobbed like a camel; he felt as though he were being rent in pieces; and when he came to himself he felt as though words had been written on his heart. And when Abu Bakr, "he who would have sacrificed father and moth-

---

\* That is, the Mirage of the Desert.

† Sura xxiv., 39, 40. See Muir, vol. iii., p. 308; and Deutsch, "Islam," in *Quarterly Review*, No. 254, p. 346.

er for Mohammed," burst into tears at the sight of the Prophet's whitening hair, "Yes," said Mohammed, "Hud and its sisters, the Terrific Suras, have turned it white before its time."*

But in order to make the general outline of Mohammed's system, which I am attempting to draw, as little imperfect as it is possible for me to make it within the limits I have prescribed myself, it is necessary to touch upon three difficult questions, which have acquired different degrees of prominence at successive periods in the history of Mohammedanism—questions which have been much misunderstood, and sometimes intentionally misrepresented, and which call more loudly even than other matters which we have been considering for a laborious investigation and a candid judgment. They need also above all things the historical sense, which does not apply the standard of the nineteenth century to the seventh, of Europeans to Asiatics, or of a high civilization to semi-barbarism; and which is content to balance the evil against the good, without requiring a verdict either for an absolute acquittal or an uncompromising condemnation. The three questions I refer to are the relation of Mohammedanism to Miracles, to Fatalism, and to wars for the sake of Religion. I

---

* Suras xi., Hud; lvi., "The Inevitable;" ci., "The Striking." See Muir, vol. ii., p. 88.

propose in the remainder of this Lecture to deal with these in succession; not I hope consciously shirking any difficulty, or glossing over what is unquestionably bad, but, of course, not professing in any degree to exhaust the subject.

I. First, then, Miracles. Mohammedanism is a system in many respects unique, but in none more so than in this, that alone of the great religions of the world it does not, in its authoritative documents, rest its claims to reception upon miracles; and yet the attitude of Mohammed toward the miraculous has been made the ground by different people of very conflicting accusations. Superficial observers up to the middle of the last century, and Christian missionaries of later times, whose zeal has not always been tempered by accurate knowledge of their subject, fastening on the fantastic character of the few miracles attributed to Mohammed by the pious credulity of his followers or the " successors," have triumphantly torn the mask from the "impostor;" and have gone on to contrast, as well they might from their point of view, the purposeless character and impossibility of his supposed miracles with the sober nature and the moral purpose which underlie the miracles of the New Testament, however supernatural they may be. Other writers — White in his " Bampton Lectures," and Paley in his " Evidences of

Christianity," and Butler in his "Analogy"—preferring to appeal to what Mohammed said of himself, rather than what was said of him by others, have driven home the contrast between Mohammedanism and Christianity by pointing out that Christianity is attested by supernatural manifestations, and is therefore divine, while Mohammedanism is neither the one nor the other. Let us inquire what the Koran itself, the only reliable authority on the subject, says, and then make one or two remarks on the general question.

In the thirteenth Sura we read:

"The unbelievers say, Unless a sign be sent down with him from his Lord, we will not believe. But thou art a preacher only, O Mohammed!"

Mohammed replies that God alone can work miracles; and, after specifying some of them, he says:

"God alone knoweth that which is hidden, and that which is revealed. He is the Great and the Most High."

In the seventh Sura the infidels ask why Mohammed had not been sent with miracles, like previous prophets? Because, replied Mohammed, miracles had proved inadequate to convince. Noah had been sent with signs, and with what effect? Where was the lost tribe of Thamud? They had refused to receive the preaching of the prophet Saled unless he showed them a sign, and caused the rock to bring forth a living camel. He did what they asked. In scorn they had cut off the camel's feet, and then, daring the Prophet to fulfill his threats of judgment, were found dead in their beds next morning, stricken by the angel of the Lord. There are some seventeen places in the Koran in which Mohammed is challenged to work a sign, and he answers them all to the same effect.

There are in the whole of the Sacred Book only two supposed exceptions to the attitude thus assumed by him; and those who know how large a part the Miraj, or miraculous journey on the Borak,* bears in popular conceptions of Mohammedanism, will learn with surprise, if they have not gone much into the matter, that there is only one passage in the Koran which can be tortured into an allusion to the journey to heaven:

"Praise be to Him who transferred his servant by night from the sacred temple to one that is more remote."†

To make this refer at all to the Miraj, we have to insert the word "Mecca" in one place, and "Jerusalem" or "seventh heaven" in another, and this, though in the sixtieth verse of the same Sura Mohammed tells us he

---

* "Borak" after all means only Lightning: the Barak of the Jews; the Barca of the Carthaginians.

† Sura xvii., 1.

was not sent with miracles, because people would not believe them; and in the sixty-second verse express mention is made of a vision he had had, beyond doubt of this very journey! So, too, in the verse, " The hour hath approached, and the moon hath been split in sunder :"* people were so anxious to see an allusion to the extravagant story of the moon's descending on the Kaaba, and entering Mohammed's sleeve, that they forgot that " the hour" means " the hour of judgment," and that the tense used is the prophetic preterite. To the eye of the Semitic "nabi," whether Jewish or Arab, the future is as the past.†

Without discussing the question of miracles at length, I would make three remarks on the general subject: First, that in a new religion the real cause for wonder is, not that it claims to be founded on miracles, but that it should ever be able to profess to do without them. In certain stages of the human mind there is no natural phenomenon which will not bear a supernatural interpretation. In fact, the supernatural is then the rule; the natural, the exception. Gibbon, I think, has somewhere asked whether there exists a single instance in

---

* Sura liv., 1.

† Cf. the past tense used in Sura xcviii., called "The Victory: "Verily, we *have* won for thee an undoubted victory"—believed to point to the conquest of Mecca two years later.

ecclesiastical history of a Father of the Church claiming for himself the power of working miracles, and I am not aware that the question has ever been answered in the affirmative. And yet we know that during many centuries there was hardly a Father of the Church who did not have miracles attributed to him by other men of equal, or even greater, reputed sanctity. Among many others, I need only mention the names of St. Benedict and St. Martin of Tours, of St. Bernard and St. Francis of Assisi. They attribute even to inanimate remains, and to relics, which were often fictitious, powers which they would never dream of claiming for themselves. St. Augustine, whose honesty is above suspicion, tells us gravely that he had ascertained, on certain evidence, that some small fragments of the disinterred relics of St. Stephen had, in his own diocese, within two years, performed no less than seventy miracles, and three of them raisings from the dead! St. Bernard was believed by his admirers to have excommunicated some flies which teased him, and "they straightway fell down in heaps." And if such be the mental atmosphere of a Church in its adolescence, *à fortiori* will an age which is capable of producing or receiving a new religion throw a mystic halo of supernaturalism around the supreme objects of its reverence. Even if the founder himself disclaims the power of working miracles, they will be thrust upon him in the most perfect good faith by the warm imagination of his disciples.

Second, and what would seem to follow from the first: In proportion as exact knowledge advances, the sphere of the supernatural is narrowed; and therefore a proof which is fitted for an imaginative and creative age is not best suited for a critical and scientific one.' Many minds, no doubt, will always crave the supernatural, and they will always find plenty of it; but to many, also, in an age like this, miracles have been a stumbling-block, and have seemed a reason for rejecting the religion which is made to rest mainly on them. Where there is a choice, it is at least wise to select the strongest ground we have; nor is there any fear that Science will ever explain too much. Behind what she explains there will always remain the unexplained and the unexplainable. Let her classify and explain the phenomena of Mind and Matter as she will, but will she ever be able to tell us what Mind and Matter are themselves? Let her analyze the springs of human action, and dissect the complex anatomy of the human conscience; but the religious instinct will still remain, as an ultimate fact of human nature; and that instinct will find without, or supply from its own resources, the verities with which it deals—the verities which supplement and explain to it the facts of Nature, and are not explained by them; which assure us that this life is not the only life, nor death extinction; and that love, the main source of human happiness, is not given us to make all real happiness impossible; which, in a word, supply the soul with the supreme objects for its worship and its aspirations.

Third: I would remark that the answers given by Mohammed himself to those who demanded miracles—that God gave the power of working miracles to whom he pleased; that other prophets had wrought miracles, and had not been believed; that he who could not know even himself adequately could not know what God had hidden; that there were greater miracles in Nature than any which could be wrought outside of it; that the Koran itself was a miracle—find at least one line of thought in a greater than Mohammed, which is not opposed to, but identical with them. People have raised questions about the authenticity and meaning of much that is in the Gospels, but, by the rules of all critical interpretation, what they can least question is the genuineness and accuracy of those passages which the Disciples have, in their undoubted honesty, recorded, as it were, in spite of themselves, and which appear to run counter to other and loftier conceptions of that majestic character on whose partially preserved utterances all

Christendom still hangs.  He who said he could of his own self do nothing; it was the Spirit which quickened —the flesh profiteth nothing; the words that he spake unto them, they were spirit and they were life; he who, when his disciples wondered at the withered fig-tree, told them that the trust in God which underlay his act would enable even them to do greater things; who, we are told, *could* not, in certain places, work miracles because of their unbelief; and when people declined to accept his teaching on higher grounds, told them, with a touch of scorn, that they might do so if they liked on the lower ground, for "his *very* works' sake;" and, lastly, who said it was an evil and adulterous generation which sought after a sign, and that no sign should be given it; and that if a man believed not Moses and the Prophets, not even would he repent though one arose from the dead: in one aspect, at all events, his teaching agreed with the Arabian Prophet whom Christians have so much discredited.  He, at all events, treated the miraculous as subordinate to the moral evidences of his mission, and struck upon a vein of thought and touched a chord of feeling which, it seems to me, is reconcilable at once with the onward march of Science and all the admitted weaknesses of human nature.*

---

* Compare throughout "Literature and Dogma," caps. v. and vi., especially p. 129, 154.

II. Second, Fatalism. I have spoken above of the extraordinary impulse given to the earlier followers of Mohammed by their vivid sense of God's personal presence with them. Inspiring, indeed, this principle then was; for it must never be forgotten, as I hope. now to prove, that the belief in an absolute predestination, which turns men into mere puppets, and all human life into a grim game of chess, wherein men are the pieces, moved by the invisible Hand of but a single Player, and which is now so general in Mohammedan countries, was, all appearances to the contrary, no part of the creed of the Prophet himself or of his immediate successors;* and I venture, therefore, to think that Gibbon is wrong in tracing the desperate valor of the primitive Mussulmans mainly to the notion that since there was no chance, there need be no fear: the germ, indeed, of fatalism was there, but its effects were as yet any thing but fatalistic.

It is of course true that there are many passages in the Koran which assert in the strongest way the foreknowledge of God. For instance, " The fate of every man have we bound about his neck;" and the relations of the slain at the battle of Ohud are comforted by the assurance that every one must die at his appointed time,

---

* Cf. *National Review* for July, 1858, p. 154.

whether it be in his own bed or on the field of battle. Nor is it possible to any religion to reconcile the conflicting dogmas of the foreknowledge of God and of the free-will of man. The New Testament does not try to do so. Most assuredly our own Articles of Religion, however successful they may be in finding a compromise between opposing views on other things, fail to effect a compromise here. Press to its logical result either the omnipotence or the omniscience of God, and what becomes of man's free-will? But logic is not the only criterion of truth, nor is it the only rule of life; and consequently there is hardly a religion which does not, in words at all events, assert as strongly as possible God's foreknowledge; in acts, at all events, man's freedom. Sometimes one will be the more prominent, sometimes the other.

The Prophet of Arabia naturally dwelt most on those attributes of God which, throwing the widest gulf between the Creator and his creatures, would, once and for all, rescue the Arabs from worshiping what their own hands had made.* He inculcates hope in adversity and humility in success, on the ground that there is a supreme Ruler who never leaves the helm; who knows what is really best for man when man himself

---

* Cf. Gobineau, "Les Religions et les Philosophies dans l'Asie Centrale." See the whole passage on this subject, p. 72, 73.

does not; and whose supreme will and power, where he asserts them, can not be crossed by the efforts of the creatures of his hand. But this is not the only side to his teaching. He asserts that man is a free agent—free to refuse or to accept the divine message; responsible for his acts, and therefore deserving, now of punishment, now of reward. The future, in fact, is in his own hands, and Mohammed incessantly urges him to use his opportunities. Ali, the most saintly, I would almost say the most Christian, of all Mussulmans, pronounces those who say the will is not free to be heretics.* There are at least four sects among Mohammedans that differ from one another on the one point of predestination and free-will. One of them, the Mutazalites, almost assert what philosophers have called the "liberty of indifference;" and there is little doubt that Mohammed himself, if the alternative had been clearly presented to him, would have had more in common with Pelagius than with Augustine, with Arminius than with Calvin.

It is difficult to believe that if Mohammed had been the consistent fatalist he is often represented to have been, he would have made prayer one of the four practical duties enjoined upon the Faithful, and that on an

---

* Quoted by Gobineau, loc. cit.

equal or even a higher footing than almsgiving, fasting, and pilgrimage.    He is said to have called it the Pillar of Religion and the Key of Paradise.    He told a tribe which, after its conversion, begged for a remission of some of the daily prayers enjoined upon them, that there could be no good in the religion in which there was no prayer; and, according to one of his successors, prayer of itself lifts men half way to heaven.    Now, if all events are absolutely fixed by the divine will and foreseen by the divine mind, then there is no possibility, I do not say of altering the fixed laws of Nature— for that is a power which few would claim for prayer— but even of a man's improving in the smallest degree, by any acts or petitions of his, his own spiritual condition.    Prayer would thus be a superfluity and delusion if explained in any other way than as an aspiration of the heart toward God, which, being an end in itself, necessarily brings its own answer with it.    Now, whether this last is a true view of prayer or not, it was certainly not Mohammed's view.    In neither case would he have been quite a consistent fatalist; but it is not likely that he could have overlooked the glaring inconsistencies involved between an absolute predestination, on the one hand, and material answers to prayer on the other.    The prayers that he enjoined five times a day[*]

---

[*] It is worth noticing, in passing, that the five daily prayers, like the

are still offered with full confidence in their efficacy by all devout Mussulmans; and the cry of the Muezzin, before daybreak, from a myriad mosques and minarets— "Prayer is better than sleep, prayer is better than sleep"—is a living witness, wherever the influence of the Prophet of Arabia has extended, more vivid than the letter of the Koran itself—overpowering even the lethargy and quietism of the East—to Mohammed's belief in God's providential government of the world, and in the freedom of man's will.

Mohammed, on one occasion, complains of the Jews that "if good fortune betide them, they say it is from God; if evil betide them, they say it is from Mohammed:" say rather, he suggests, all is from God. But what, he asks in the very next verse, has come to these people that they are not near to understanding what is told them?

"Whatever good betideth thee is from God, and whatever betideth thee of evil is from thyself."*

There are the two contradictories brought face to face, and left fronting one another for all time; and can any religion do more, and perhaps I may add less, than this?

---

rite of circumcision, though universally observed by Mussulmans, are not enjoined in the Koran itself. Circumcision is not even mentioned in the Koran: it is one of the many Pre-Islamitic practices which Mohammed tacitly sanctioned.

* Sura iv., 80, 81.

It is not difficult to see how one and the same doctrine of God's foreknowledge, on the one hand, and of his actual intervention in human affairs on the other, may have diametrically opposite effects in different natures, or in even the same natures under different circumstances.

> "There is a tide in the affairs of men
> Which, taken at the flood, leads on to fortune;
> Omitted, all the voyage of their life
> Is bound in shallows and in miseries."

The early Mussulmans, in the new burst of life breathed into them by Mohammed, it inspired with double energy and double enthusiasm, as in their best days it inspired the Puritans, the Covenanters, the Pilgrim Fathers. But to their descendants in their more normal state—the lethargic Soufy, the brooding Sepoy, the insensate Turk; I would add, to those religious people who refuse to prevent the miseries and the diseases which Nature they think has attached to guilt—it furnishes with a new excuse for that life of inactivity to which they are already too much disposed, since they believe that they are acquiescing, as in duty bound, in the immutable decrees of God.*

III. One more question remains to be discussed in this Lecture—the wars of Islam, and the relation they bear

---

* See an eloquent passage on this subject in an article of the *National Review* for October, 1861, entitled "The Great Arabian," p. 312.

to Mohammed's religion. It is true that it was not till
the Prophet found himself, to his surprise, in a position
of power at Medina, that we hear even a whisper of
the sword as an instrument of conversion. It is then,
and not till then, that we are told that other prophets
have been sent by God to attest his different attributes
in their own person and by their miraculous acts; but
that men had closed their eyes to the character and denied the miracles even of Moses and of Christ. What
remained to the last of the prophets except that he
should try the last argument of the sword? Was the
sword then an after-thought and an accidental append-
age merely to Mohammed's religion, or was it an essential part? I am inclined to think that the nature of the
case itself and the verdict of subsequent experience will
tend to show that, however absent it was from Mohammed's thoughts at first, and however alien to his gentle
and forgiving nature, it came in the progress of events,
to some extent in his own life, and still more so in the
lives of his successors, to be the latter. How this came
about requires careful explanation.

Mohammed's notion of God had never been that of
a great moral Being who designs that the creatures he
has created should, from love and gratitude to him, become one with him, or even assimilated to him. Mohammed believed in God, feared, reverenced, and obey-

ed him after his light, as few Jews or Christians ever
did; but he could hardly be said in the Christian, or
even the Jewish sense of the word, to love God.  It is
possible that repeated acts of obedience to a God whom
he always represents as compassionate and merciful
might imply or result in love; but at all events with
him love was not, as it is in Christianity, the fulfilling
of the law, the inspiring motive to action, the sum of
its theology as of its morality.  Had it been so, Mohammed would have seen more reason to doubt whether the sword could ever be its best ally; but though he
must in any case have seen that it was impossible to
force men to love God, it may have crossed his mind
that it was possible to force men to abstain from idolatry, to acknowledge one God with their lips, to fear
and to obey him at all events in their outward acts.

Had Mohammed remained master of himself — had
he remained, that is to say, the simple Prophet throughout his career—it is possible, on the one hand, that his
message would never have spread in his lifetime beyond the walls of Mecca and Medina; and it is more
than probable, on the other, that his character might
now be held up to the world as that which we feel the
founder of a religion ought to be; that which Confucius and Buddha were, and that which Mohammed
himself, throughout his life at Mecca, unquestionably

was—a perfect model of the saintly virtues. There is one glory of the founder of a religion, another of the founder of a nation, another of the founder of an empire. They are better kept distinct; and the limits of the human faculties are an adequate security against their being often found united in one person. It is the uncongenial mixture of earthly needs and heavenly aspirations which has made Mohammed at once a smaller and a greater man—at once more and less commanding than he would otherwise have been. What he gains as a ruler of men, he loses as a guide and as an example; and people are, naturally enough, led to condemn the prophet for the drastic energy of the leader, and the leader for the shortcomings of the prophet. It is, perhaps, inevitable that Christians should do so; for the image of Him whose kingdom was not of this world, who did not strive nor cry, whose servants were never to draw the sword in his defense, forces itself upon the mind, in silent and reproachful antithesis to the mixed and sullied character of the Prophet-soldier Mohammed. The trumpet-call is not the still, small voice; it is immeasurably below it: but there has been room for both in the development of humanity.

Now, on a sudden, Mohammed found himself in a position he had not courted, which was forced on him by his enemies; and the exigencies of his exiled fol-

lowers—the need of sustenance, the appetite for plunder, the desire of revenge, and the longing for their
homes, no less than the impending attack of the Koreishites—drove the Prophet for the first time to place
himself at their head; and, for temporal purposes only,
to unsheath the sword. Mohammed thus became a general by accident; and the extraordinary success of his
first ventures deepened the impression, already half
natural to an Arab, that the sword might be a legitimate instrument of spiritual warfare, and that God had
put into his power a new means, where all other means,
as in the case of previous prophets, had failed. At all
events the sword, originally drawn for temporal purposes only, was found to have, half unexpectedly, answered another end as well. It was found that the religion, once started by the sword, was soon able to throw
the sword away. The march of the Faith anticipated
the march of the army of the Faithful, and the all but
uniform success of the armies, when they had to fight,
seemed to stamp the means used with the divine ap-
probation; and so it was that Mohammed felt less and
less scruple as to the use of the sword where it seemed
to him to be wanted; and at the close of his life, in one
of the last Suras of the Koran, we are hardly surprised
to find the stern command and the " magnificent pre-
sentiment:"

" Fight on, therefore, till there be no temptation to idolatry, and the religion becomes God's alone."*

The early Kaliphs obeyed the precepts and imitated the example of the warrior-Prophet, and went forth on their enterprise in all the plenitude of autocratic power ; there was no rivalry between Church and State to tie their hands, for the Kaliph was the head of both in one ; the State, so far as it had any separate existence at all, being simply a creature of the Church. And let us here turn aside for a moment to examine the relation then subsisting between the spiritual and temporal power, first in the Western, and then in the Eastern Empire, and to contrast it with the extraordinary concentration of all the energies of a new-born enthusiasm placed in the hands of the Kaliph. We shall then see, on the one hand, from what a vantage-ground the Arabs, at that precise moment, entered the lists to contend with Christendom ; but, on the other, we shall note how few are the men and how rare the occasions on which power of any kind can afford to dispense with those checks which are a condition of its permanence, and which alone can prevent it from developing into unbridled tyranny or dying of inanition.

The Christianity of the West then had, centuries be-

---

* Sura viii., 40. Cf. also xxii., 40, and ix., *passim :* perhaps the last Sura Mohammed composed.

fore this, organized an *imperium in imperio* which afforded a substantial check to the tyranny of the emperors, and, by its moral majesty, could restrain a savage barbarian even in the full career of conquest. Ambrose had sternly rebuked Theodosius; Innocent had mitigated the horrors of the sack of Rome by Alaric; Leo had turned back Attila, and half disarmed Genseric. The transference of the seat of empire to Constantinople forced the Bishops of Rome into a political prominence which would not otherwise have belonged to them; and, in process of time, the spiritual power thus fortified began to contend, on something like equal terms, with the temporal. Gregory the Great, whose pontificate ended shortly before the " call " of the Prophet of Arabia, was the virtual sovereign of Rome, able to protect it alike from the ferocity of the Lombards and from the pretentious weakness of the Exarchs. Before long the sacerdotal monarchs who reigned on the Tiber were to be seen deposing by right divine one Frankish dynasty which ruled upon the Rhine; setting up another of their own creation; and, finally, in the person of Charles the Great, giving new body to the phantom of the ancient Roman Empire which had never ceased to flit before the mind of Europe, and fancying, in their superb audacity, that a breath might overthrow what a breath had made. And by the

time that the Eternal City itself heard the dreaded
Tecbir at their gates, it was to a Pope and not a Cæsar—a Pope, too, elected in hot haste, without even the
formal sanction of the Cæsar—that Rome owed her
safety!*

But the religion of the Eastern Empire, to quote
Gibbon's epigram, could teach men only " to suffer and
to yield." The Patriarch of Constantinople, unlike the
Patriarch of Rome, was the puppet of the emperor, indorsed his worst deeds, or was swept away if he ob-
jected to them.† And the Saracens who besieged the
ceremonious Emperor of the East in his own capital
must have enjoyed, if they could read, the form of
service, prescribed by Church and State together, for
the day on which the emperor should trample on the
necks of the captive Mussulmans, while the singers
were to chant, " Thou hast made mine enemies my
footstool," and the people were to shout forty times
the " Kyrie Eleeson."‡ The crusading spirit which

---

* Leo IV.

† See the history of the Iconoclastic Emperors generally, A.D. 717–841,
and their dealings with the Patriarchs of Constantinople. Read especially,
on the one hand, the account of the dastardly submission of the Patriarch
Anastasius to Leo, and, on the other, the horrible cruelties inflicted on
the Patriarch Constantine by Copronymus. Milman, vol. ii., chap. vii.

‡ See the " De Ceremoniis Aulæ et Ecclesiæ Byzantinæ " of Constantine Porphyrogenitus, vol. ii., p. 19 ; quoted by Gibbon, chap. liii., p. 116,
and note.

might have been evoked by a proposition of the great Emperors, Nicephorus and Zimisces, to give a martyr's crown to those who fell in battle with the infidels, was checkmated by a counter-proposition of the Patriarch to exclude from the highest rites of the Church all those who took up arms, even in self-defense.* Had it been otherwise, the period of the Crusades might have been anticipated by more than a hundred years. We see, therefore, that in the West, by the time that the tide of Arab conquest had spread from Mecca to Gibraltar, the spiritual power was independent of temporal, and was often able to control or neutralize its action, even in temporal affairs; while in the East, on which the storm was first to burst, it was almost non-existent; and if ever it did cause its voice to be heard, the cry it uttered was that of Phocion, not of Demosthenes — of Jeremiah, not of Isaiah: that of submission to the inevitable, not of resistance to the bitter end.

But with the Saracens the case was different. The God of Mohammed, like the God of the wanderers of the wilderness, and unlike the God of Christendom, was pre-eminently the God of battles. The early Mussulmans shed tears when held back within their leashes from the battle; and the Emperor Leo, who condemned

---

* See Gibbon, loc. cit.

the Mohammedan idea of God, must have secretly envied the vigor that it brought. Military zeal under a
tried leader is a strong passion, so is religious enthusiasm; and never probably in the history of the world
have these two passions burned with so consuming a
flame as they did in the breasts of the early followers
of Mohammed. The civil, the religious, and the military were as indissolubly blended together in his system as they were in mediæval chivalry. It was not so
much religion that became warlike, as war, the normal
condition of the Arabs on a small scale, now itself
became religious, with the whole world for its battle-
ground. Probably in no army in the world, not even
among the Scotch Covenanters, nor among Cromwell's
Ironsides, did religious exercises so form part of the
military discipline, and religious enthusiasm so infuse
an *esprit de corps.*

The early battles of Islam—Bedr and Ohud, Kadesia
and Nehavend, the Yermuk and Aiznadin; its early
sieges—Bozra and Damascus, Jerusalem and Aleppo,
Memphis and Alexandria—are more than Homeric in
the reckless valor and the chivalrous devotion that they
exhibit. And it is to be remembered that they are in
the main historical. Kaled is the Achilles of the siege
of Damascus, Amrou of that of Memphis, Dames of
Aleppo. At Bedr, Omeir, a mere stripling, who, fear-

ing that he might be rejected on account of his youth, had managed to join the small army of the Faithful unknown to Mohammed, flung away the dates he was eating with the vow that he would eat the next in the presence of God. " Paradise is before you, the devil and hell-fire in your rear," was the exhortation of the generals at the battle of Yermuk. The Faithful courted death with the ecstasy of martyrs, and received a martyr's reward. At Aiznadin, Derar maintained a flying fight single-handed against thirty infidels, and killed seventeen of their number. At the siege of Damascus, a Saracen heroine, who had followed her husband, Aban, to the holy war, saw him killed by her side, stopped to bury him, and then fought on in the post of danger till she slew the famous archer who had killed her husband. Nor is there any period in the history of Mohammedanism, late or early, in which the intensity of the crusading spirit does not on occasion manifest itself. It is God's battle that each Mussulman is fighting, and as God may will, he is ready for either event—for victory or defeat, for life or death. In the Crusades themselves, when Christendom seemed to be seized with a double portion of the Mohammedan spirit, by the confession of the Christians, the generosity, the reckless valor, the self-sacrifice, and the chivalry were not all on one side.

Richard of England and Frederick Barbarossa found their match in Saladin; and even the history of England's empire in India teems with proofs that the vital spark of fanaticism is latent only, not extinct.

Whenever hitherto in the history of Mohammedanism the belief has grown feeble that the Faithful hold a commission from on high to put down evil, wherever it shows itself, with a strong hand, it must be admitted that the religion itself has proportionately failed to do its proper work, both as a compelling and as a restraining power.  In the Middle Ages the vitality and energy of Mohammedanism evidenced itself most clearly, not in Arabia or Persia or Africa, where its success was most complete, but in the Christian border lands—in Spain, in Palestine, in Asia Minor—where the crusading spirit was most evoked.  Where there was no outlet for an active and even a material warfare, against what was believed to be evil, there corruption crept in, and stealthily paralyzed all the energies of Mussulman society.  "*Corruptio optimi fit pessima.*"  Ommiade and Abbasside and Fatimite Kaliphs; Ghaznevide and Seljukian and Ottoman Sultans, passed through the same dreary stages of luxury and decay; and the government that now represents, or misrepresents, the Kaliphate, and is by most people foolishly supposed to be the main support of Islam, originally, in the hands of men like Abu Bakr or Omar, the best, the simplest, and the most republican of all absolute governments, has, in the hands of the Ottoman Turks, ever since their faith ceased to be militant, become the most hopeless of despotisms, since the abject submission to the ruler remains, while all reason for submission has vanished.*

In the eyes of many the admission I have frankly made that the propagation of religion by the sword has been an essential part of Mohammedanism will serve to condemn it at once, and so in the abstract and from the highest point of view it ought. The sword is a rough surgical instrument in any case; but the doctrine that religion can ever be propagated by it, paradoxical as it sounds now, has seemed a truism in more ages than one; and though the Arabs were semi-barbarians, the conquered nations were constrained to admit that in their conquests they were not barbarous. Their wars were not mere wars of devastation, like those of Alaric or Genseric in earlier times, or of Zenghis Khan or Tamerlane in later. It was the savage boast of Attila, the genius of destruction, the "scourge of God," that the grass never grew where his horse had once trodden.

* See this line of thought developed by Maurice, "Religions of the World," p. 29, seq. I have done little more in this paragraph than condense and illustrate his argument.

But of the Mohammedan conquests it would rather be true to say that, after the first wave of invasion had swept by, two blades of grass were found growing where one had grown before; like the thunderstorm, they fertilized while they destroyed; and from one end of the then known world to the other, with their religion they sowed seeds of literature, of commerce, and of civilization. And as these disappeared, in the lapse of years, in one part of the Mussulman world, they reappeared in another. When they died out, with the dying of the Abbasside Kaliphate, along the banks of the Tigris and Euphrates, they revived again on the Guadalquivir and Guadiana. To the splendors and civilization of Damascus succeeded Bagdad; to Bagdad, Cairo; to Cairo, Cordova.

Mohammedanism has been accused of hostility to the growth of the human intellect. It may have been so in its earliest days, when Omar, as the story goes, condemned the Alexandrian Library to the flames by his famous dilemma: "If these books agree with the Book of God, they are useless; if they disagree, they are pernicious; and in either case they must be destroyed." It may be so whenever there is a passing outburst of fanaticism; but it is not so in its essential nature, nor has it been so historically, not even in its wars. The religion which has declared that " the ink of the learned is as precious as the blood of the martyrs,"* and which declares that at the Day of Decision a special account will be given of the use made of the intellect, can not fairly be accused of obscurantism. It was not so when, during the darkest period of European history, the Arabs for five hundred years held up the torch of learning to humanity. It was the Arabs who then "called the Muses from their ancient seats;" who collected and translated the writings of the Greek masters; who understood the geometry of Apollonius, and wielded the weapons found in the logical armory of Aristotle. It was the Arabs who developed the sciences of Agriculture and Astronomy, and created those of Algebra and Chemistry; who adorned their cities with colleges and libraries, as well as with mosques and palaces; who supplied Europe with a school of philosophers from Cordova, and a school of physicians from

---

* Quoted by Gobineau, p. 26. So, too, Abulpharagius, in his "Dynasties," says that Almamun, Kaliph of Bagdad, invited learned men to his court because they were the elect of God, whose lives were devoted to the development of the mind. (See Gibbon, vol. vii., p. 34.) Against the destruction of the Alexandrian Library by Omar may fairly be set the destruction by the Crusaders of an immense library at Tripoli, in Palestine. The general, finding that the first room of the library contained the Koran only, ordered the whole library to be burned. So, too, Cardinal Ximenes, on entering the Moorish capital, showed that a crass fanaticism is not the prerogative of one religion only, by his order to destroy the vast collection of Arabic MSS. there, with the exception of three hundred medical works, which he reserved for his own university.

Salerno. When we condemn the Mohammedan wars, let us at least remember what of good they brought with them.

Nor is Mohammedanism the only religion which has tried to propagate itself by the sword. It is true, of course, that a holy war waged by Christians is in direct contravention of the spirit of their Founder, while one waged by Mohammedans is in accordance with both the practice and the precept of the Prophet, and so far there is no parallel at all between the two religions. The means authorized by Christ for the spread of his religion were moral and spiritual only. The means authorized by Mohammed were persuasion and example first; but, failing these, the sword.

Yet, historically speaking, the contrast between the practice of Christians and Mohammedans has not been so sharp as is often supposed. The Saxon wars of Charles the Great were avowedly religious wars, and differed chiefly from the Syrian wars of Omar and of Ali, from the African wars of Amrou and Akbah, and the Spanish wars of Moussa and of Tarik, in that they were much more protracted and vastly less successful. Otto the Great, the best of Charles's successors, used the sword with vigor to extend the external profession of Christianity among the Sclavonian tribes who dwelt along the shores of the Baltic. The Mediæval Papacy, whatever its other services to progress, was never backward to unfurl the standard of a religious war, whether against the common enemy of Christendom, or, as more often happened, against a sect of heretics—the Albigenses or the Waldenses—nearer home. Nor, in point of ferocity, is it clear that religious wars waged by Christians will compare favorably with those of Mohammedans. The Mohammedan wars were never internecine. Even on the field of battle the conquering Mussulman allowed his conquered foe the two other alternatives of conversion or of tribute. When Abu Bakr first invaded Syria, he charged his troops not to mutilate the dead, not to slay old men, women, or children, not to cut down fruit-trees, not to kill cattle unless they were needed for food; and these humane precepts served like a code of laws of war during the career of Mohammedan conquest. And this, be it remembered, among Orientals, who had always been remarkable for their disregard of human life. When we remember, on the other hand, the massacre of four thousand five hundred pagan Saxons in cold blood by Charles the Great —when we remember the famous answer by which the Papal Legate, in the Albigensian war, quieted the scruples of a too conscientious general, "Kill all; God will know his own"—when we recall the Spanish Inquisition, the conquest of Mexico and Peru, the massacre of St. Bartholomew, and the sack of Magdeburg by Tilly, we shall be disposed, never, indeed, to justify religious wars, but to point out that, of the religious wars which the world has seen, the Mohammedan are certainly not the worst—in their object, in their methods, or in their results.

Nor is the extermination of moral evil in all cases an unworthy object of war. There are occasions even in our modern civilization, and in an era of non-intervention, when one longs to feel that the sword a nation wields may be, in their eyes at all events, the sword of the Lord and of Gideon. An unselfish war to put down the slave-trade or the opium-traffic, to counteract some "Holy Alliance" of emperors against the rights of peoples, to prevent a giant iniquity like the partition of Poland, is perhaps the only kind of war, except those of self-defense, to which the spirit of Christianity is not opposed. Christianity *is* opposed to wars of aggression, to dynastic wars, and, above all, to religious wars; for a religious war rests upon the irreligious assumption that one fallible man holds a fiat from Omnipotence to step between another human soul and God; and to enforce his partial views of truth upon a fellow-mortal, who, for aught he knows, may have as wide a prospect and as deep an insight as he has himself. *"Deorum injuriæ Deis curæ."* The sword may silence; it can not convince: it may enforce hypocrisy; it can never force belief. But this has not always seemed so self-evident; and I say it deliberately and with all the force of conviction, compared with the war of the Confederate States in the nineteenth century for the perpetuation of slavery, compared with England's Japanese wars for the extension of her trade, her Chinese wars for the sale of her opium, and her miserable African wars waged for the possession of a territory which she bought, and had no moral right to buy, from those who sold what they had no moral right to sell,* the Mohammedan wars for the propagation of a comparatively pure religion and a higher morality were, in their time and according to their light, inasmuch as they were not purely selfish, I do not say excusable, but they were at least intelligible and natural.

Here I must close this Lecture. What of good and what of evil the world owes to Mohammed; what is the condition and what the prospects of Mohammedanism now; what, as a matter of fact, is the historical connection between Mohammedanism and Christianity —its points of difference as well as of resemblance; finally, and most important of all, how that connection ought to be regarded by Christians, and under what

* See Appendix to Lecture III.

conditions or modifications the two great creeds may work together, or, if needs be, apart, for their common object, the general good of humanity—these are some of the points I hope to be able to discuss in my fourth and concluding Lecture.

# LECTURE IV.

MARCH 7, 1874.

## MOHAMMEDANISM AND CHRISTIANITY.

Say unto the Christians, their God and my God is one.—THE KORAN.

'Ο δὲ 'Ιησοῦς εἶπε, Μὴ κωλύετε αὐτόν· ὃς γὰρ οὐκ ἔστι καθ' ἡμῶν, ὑπὲρ ἡμῶν ἐστιν.—ST. MARK.

IT may have been observed that in attempting, in my last Lecture, to deal with some of the questions connected with Mohammedanism—such as miracles, fatalism, religious wars—which have much perplexed the Christian mind, I omitted to say any thing on a point which, more even than any of these, has scandalized those who view Mohammedanism from a distance: I mean the notions Mohammedans have formed of a future state. The omission was not altogether accidental, for I am inclined to think that too much stress has been laid upon these notions, no less by Mohammed's apologists than by his critics; more stress than the Koran itself, and more even than the current Mohammedan belief, will warrant. But, remembering a remark of

Sprenger's* that, although Islam has been described in many books, yet educated people have not got much farther in the knowledge of it than that the Turks are Mohammedans and allow polygamy, I think it will be well to add a few words to counteract the common notion, which I should be disposed to place on a par with this, that the Paradise of the Mohammedans is nothing more than the enjoyment of polygamy, with its earthly drawbacks and limitations removed.

So much has been said and written about the gross nature of Mohammed's Paradise, the black-eyed Houris, the perfumes and the spices, with which his imagination furnished it, that ordinary people may be excused for believing that it was mainly, if not wholly, sensual. But this is not, in the main, a true, and still less is it an adequate, account of the matter. The passages are few in number in which Mohammed dwells much on these aspects of the future, and, even in these, much of what is said is explained by orthodox Mohammedans to be merely Oriental imagery, while some of it is especially suitable — the bubbling fountains and the shady gardens above all—to the inhabitants of a dry and thirsty land, such as Arabia is.†

---

* Sprenger, vol. ii., p. 18.

† See Sale's "Introduction," p. 73; and Lane's "Modern Egyptians," vol. i., p. 84.

Few people now put a literal interpretation upon the gorgeous imagery and the glowing colors used in the Book of Revelation to describe the Celestial City; and every one will admit that in all religions, even the most spiritual, the circumstances of this life must necessarily, to some extent, lend both form and color to the views of the life to come.   The Red Indian dreams of a heaven behind the cloud-topped hills, embosomed in woods, wherein his faithful dog will bear him company.   The fierce Norseman hoped to be admitted after death to the Hall of Odin, and there, reclining on a couch, to drink ale forever from the skulls of his enemies whom he had slain in battle.   The earnest Methodist pictures to himself a place

"Where congregations ne'er break up,
    And Sabbaths never end,"

for the simple reason that he finds his highest spiritual happiness in these things on earth.   A polygamous people could hardly have pictured to themselves a heaven without polygamy.   It would never even have occurred to them that such a thing was possible, since few of them had ever known a society on earth which was without it; nor do I suppose that any individual Christian who has ever known the luxury of home affection has been able to accept in any literal sense the doctrine that in the future world there are to be no exclusive attach-

ments,* for the simple reason, again, that without individual love no human heart can conceive of the possibility of any happiness as complete or real.

Again, it is to be remembered that much that is material or even gross in the Mohammedan conception of
a future life is due, not to Mohammed, but to Mohammed's successors; and it is not the least of the enigmas
that attach to the extraordinary and unique character of
the Prophet that his views of a future state are never
more spiritual than at the time when, according to the
common theory, he had most entirely, and, in fact, he
had to some extent, fallen away from his austerely moral
life. Contrast the tone of the Suras, referring to this
subject, which were written at Mecca early in his life,†
with the third, for instance, which was written at Medina
many years later.

"Fair," says he, "in the sight of men are the pleasures
of women and children; fair are the treasured treasures
of gold and silver; and fine horses; and flocks; and
corn-fields! Such is the enjoyment of this world's life.
But God! goodly is the home with him!

"Shall I tell you of better things than these, prepared
for those who fear God in his presence? Theirs shall
be gardens beneath which the rivers flow, and in which

---

* St. Matt. xxii., 30.
† Sura lv., 44–58; lvi., 17–36; lxxvi., 12–22.

they shall abide for aye, and wives of stainless purity, and acceptance with God, for God regardeth his servants.

"They who say, O our Lord, we have indeed believed, pardon our sins, and keep us from the torment of the fire.

"The patient are they and the truthful, the lowly and the charitable, and they who ask for pardon as each day breaks."*

Surely here, as elsewhere, and increasingly so as the Prophet drew near his end, it is the presence of God, the knowledge of him, the eternal Salaam or Peace with which they shall salute one another, the purity of love, and not its sensuality, which are the most prominent ideas.

Heaven and hell, indeed, were realities to the Mohammedan mind in a sense in which they have hardly ever been to any other nation. With a more than Dantesque realism, Mohammed saw the tortures of the lost no less than the bliss of the faithful.

"They shall dwell," he says, "amid burning winds and in scalding water, under the shade of a black smoke which is no shade, neither cool nor grateful, . . . and they shall surely eat of the fruit of the tree Ez-Zakkoum, and shall fill their bellies therewith, and they

---

* Sura xiii., 12–15.

shall drink thereon boiling water, even as a thirsty camel drinketh."*

And again he says:

"They shall have garments of fire fitted unto them, their bowels shall be dissolved thereby, and also their skins, and they shall be beaten with maces of iron." †

And once more, in one of his very early Suras, which, if it is memorable for nothing else, is memorable for its superb audacity, when we recollect that as yet Mohammed's prophetic claims were treated only with contemptuous indifference, and he himself was a mere outcast:

"Woe be," he says, "on that day to those who accused the prophets of imposture!

"It shall be said unto them, Go ye into that which ye denied as a falsehood.

"Go ye into the shadow of the smoke of hell, which, though it ascend in three columns,

"Shall not shade you from the heat, neither shall it be of service against the flames;

"But it shall cast forth sparks as big as towers,

"And their color shall be like unto that of red camels.

"Woe be on that day unto those who accuse the prophets of imposture." ‡

---

* Sura lvi., 41–56.　　　　　　　　　† Sura xxii., 20–21.

‡ Sura lxxvii , 29, to end.　The "Woe be," etc., is a refrain which recurs ten times in the Sura.

"What shall be our reward," asked his earliest followers of Mohammed, "if we fall in battle?" "Paradise," said the Prophet, without the slightest hesitation. In the war of Tabuk his men demurred to marching because it was harvest-time. "Your harvest, it lasts for a day," said Mohammed; "what will come of your harvest through all eternity?" They complained of the burning sun. "Hell is hotter," said the Prophet, and on they went.*

That it was desirable to dwell with so much persistence upon the enormous issues involved as regards the future life, in every act and thought of this, I am far from asserting; since self-interest, however enlightened and however refined, however even spiritualized it may be, is self-interest still. But at all events it was stern reality to Mohammed and to his followers. The future was all as real and as instant to him as it was to the Apostles when, expecting, as they did, from the interpretation they put upon Christ's words, to see him in their own lifetime coming in the clouds of heaven, they drove home their warnings by bidding men flee from "the wrath to come." In every successive crisis of the Christian Church it has been the belief of Christians

---

* Carlyle's "Heroes," p. 239; and Sura ix., 82, etc. In this expedition water was so scarce that the fainting troops were obliged to kill the camels and drink the water out of their stomachs.

that the darkest hour is that before the dawn, and it has been used, however mistakenly, yet with effect and with sincerity, to comfort the depressed, to awaken the sleeping, and to arouse the dead. "*Finem suum mundus jam non nunciat solum, sed ostendit*," says St. Gregory amid the devastations of the Lombards. "*Appropinquante jam mundi termino*," is the heading of even legal documents amid the deeper depression of the tenth century caused by the ravages of the Hungarians by land and the Norsemen by sea. This is the burden of St. Bernard's hymns, of Savonarola's preachings, of Bunyan's allegories. Truly, if Mohammed sinned at all in this respect, he sinned in good company.

But the future world, ever present though it was to the minds of the early Mohammedans, did not supply the motive by which they were really inspired. A selfish hope of heaven and a slavish fear of hell may act as a "negative stimulus"—may possibly teach passive resistance to temptation; but it does not nerve the arm to strike or quicken the eye to see. Perhaps, indeed, the highest heroism of all, that which consists in absolute conscious self-sacrifice or self-annihilation for the good of others—the heroism of the ideal just man in the second book of Plato's "Republic;" the heroism of Moses when he prayed to be blotted out of the Book that God had written; the heroism of a greater than

Moses when He died upon the cross—is impossible to those who believe firmly in a future life, the happiness or misery of which is to be exactly determined by the life here. But there may be true heroism even short of the truest; and all true heroism, even if it can not deny or forget its reward, is stimulated not so much by the reward as by the difficulty of obtaining it. The reward, to use an Aristotelian phrase, is an ἐπιγιγνόμενόν τι τέλος, something thrown in—an after-thought and accessory merely; and this is what a future life was to the primitive warriors of the Crescent.

Nor is it true, in any sense of the word, that Mohammed's is an easy or sensual religion. With its frequent fasts, its five prayers a day, its solitudes, its almsgivings, its pilgrimages, even in the tortures of Indian fakirs and the howlings of Mecca dervishes, which are the abuse, and not the use, of the religion — it certainly does not appeal much to the laziness or the sensuality or the selfishness of mankind.

In his capacity even of temporal ruler, Mohammed rarely gave material rewards to his followers. Abu Bakr, Ali, Omar, Hamza, when in his early days they ranged themselves as friends around the then friendless enthusiast, sacrificed, as it must have appeared to them, all their worldly hopes; they little thought that they were enrolling themselves in that most select band of heroes who may be said to have made History. On one occasion, late in his life, Mohammed did give some material rewards to recent and perhaps half - hearted converts, but the exception only proved the rule, and that in the most memorable manner. The Helpers of Medina were naturally dissatisfied, but Mohammed re-called them to their allegiance by words which went straight from his heart to theirs: that he had given things of the world to those who cared for such things, but to them he had given himself. Others returned home with sheep and camels, the Helpers with .the Prophet of God. Verily, if all the men of the earth went one way, and the Helpers of Medina another, he would go the way of the Helpers of Medina.* The Helpers burst into tears, and exclaimed that they were more than satisfied with what he had given them. And, just before his death, Mohammed commended these same Helpers of Medina to the protection of the exiles who had accompanied him from Mecca. "Hold in honor," said he, " the Helpers of Medina; the number of believers may increase, but that of the Helpers never can.† They were my family, and with them I found

---

* Alluded to in Sura lix., 8, 9 ; viii , 42. See Muir, vol. iv., p. 151–154.

† Cf. Herodotus, iii., 119 : ὦ βασιλεῦ, ἀνὴρ μέν μοι ἂν ἄλλος γένοιτο, εἰ δαίμων ἐθέλοι, καὶ τέκνα ἄλλα, εἰ ταῦτα ἀποβάλοιμι · πατρὸς δὲ καὶ μητρὸς οὐκ ἔτι μευ ζωόντων ἀδελφεὸς ἂν ἄλλος οὐδενὶ τρόπῳ γένοιτο. Cf. also Soph., *Antigone*, 909–912.

a home; do good to those who do good to them, and break friendship with those who are hostile to them."

Perhaps there is no remark one has heard more often about Mohammedanism than that it was so successful because it was so sensual; but there is none more destitute of truth, as if any religion could owe its permanent success to its bad morality! I do not say that its morality is perfect, or equal to the Christian morality. Mohammed did not make the manners of Arabia, and he was too wise to think that he could either unmake or remake them all at once. Solon remarked of his own legislation that his laws were not the best that he could devise, but that they were the best the Athenians could receive; and his defense has generally been accepted as a sound one. Moses took the institutions of a primitive society as he found them—the patriarchal power, internecine war, blood feuds, the right of asylum, polygamy, and slavery—and did not abolish any one of them; he only mitigated their worst evils, and so unconsciously prepared the way in some cases for their greater permanence, in others for their eventual extinction.

In like manner the religion of Christ did not sweep into oblivion any national or political institutions. He contented himself with planting principles in the hearts of his followers which would, when the time was ripe for it, work out their abolition. Willing to sow if others could reap, to labor if others could enter into his labors, he cast into the ground the grain of mustard-seed, and was content, with the eye of faith alone, to see it grow into the mighty tree whose branches should overspread the world, and whose leaves should be for the healing of the nations. With sublime self-restraint and self-sacrifice, governed by his thought for the boundless possibilities of the future of his Church, rather than by the impulse of the moment, he forbore to denounce in so many words the inveterate evils of the Roman Empire, which must have gone to his soul's soul—foreign conquest, tyranny, the amphitheatre, slavery. He even used words which have been wrongly construed to mean that at all times passive obedience is a duty, and that the people have nothing to do with the laws but to obey them. Nor has the Christian Church—sections of which have for strange and various, but intelligible, reasons canonized a Constantine and a Vladimir, a Cyril and a Charles the Great, a Dunstan and a Becket—ever attached the name of Saint to some who, in the fullness of time, have carried out far more fully and in spirit Christ's work, albeit in seeming contradiction to the letter of the law which inculcated submission to existing powers and institutions—to a Telemachus or a Theodoric, to an Alfred or a Wilberforce. And yet no Christian will deny that the monk Telemachus, who threw himself between the swords of the gladiators, and, braving the fury of the spectators athirst for blood, accomplished by his death what his life could never have won, did a deed which all the "Acta Sanctorum" could be searched to parallel.

Now Mohammed was a legislator and a statesman, as well as the founder of a religion; and why is the defense which we allow to Solon, and the praise we bestow upon the limited scope of the Mosaic legislation, denied to Islam?

Polygamy is, indeed, next to caste, the most blighting institution to which a nation can become a prey. It pollutes society at the fountain-head, for the family is the source of all political and of all social virtues. Mohammed would have more than doubled the debt of gratitude the Eastern world owes to him had he swept it away; but he could not have done so, even if he had fully seen its evils. It is not fair to represent polygamy as a part of Mohammedanism any more than it is fair to represent slavery as a part of Christianity. The one co-exists with the other without being mixed with it, even as the muddy Arve and the clear Rhone keep their currents distinct long after they have been united in one river-bed. Perhaps it is strange that they ever could have co-existed, even for a day; but we have to deal with facts as they are; and it is a fact that slavery has co-existed with Christianity—nay, has professed to justify itself by Christianity — even till this nineteenth century. Mohammed could not have made a *tabula rasa* of Eastern society, but what he could do he did. He at least put strict limitations on the unbounded license of Eastern polygamy* and the facility of Eastern divorce.† If the two social touchstones of a religion are the way in which, relatively to the time, it deals with the weaker sex, and the way in which it regards the poor and the oppressed, Mohammed's religion can stand the test.‡ He improved the condition of women by freeing them from the arbitrary patriarchal power of the parents or the heirs of their husbands, by inculcating just and kind treatment of them by their husbands themselves, by giving them legal rights in case of unfair treatment, and by absolutely prohibiting the

---

* Sura iv., 3, etc.

† Sura iv., 39 and 127 ; xxxiii., 48, 52, etc.

‡ Among many other illustrations of this see (*a*) the oath taken early in his life with other Koreishites, " to defend the oppressed so long as a drop of water remained in the ocean," an act the remembrance of which Mohammed said " he would not exchange for the choicest camel in Arabia ;" (*b*) the account given by Jafar to the Najashy of Abyssinia of the change wrought by Mohammed among his followers ; perhaps the noblest and truest summary we have of the moral teaching of the Prophet ; (*c*) the pledge of Acaba, A. D. 621, taken by his first converts from Medina ; (*d*) Sura ii., 170 : " There is no piety in turning your faces toward the East or the West, but he is pious who believeth in God ; . . . who for the love of God distributeth his wealth to his kindred, and to the orphans, and the needy, and the wayfarer."

incestuous marriages which were rife in the times of ignorance, and the still more horrible practice of the burying alive of female infants.*   Nor was this all, for besides imposing restrictions on polygamy, by his severe laws at first, and by the strong moral sentiment aroused by these laws afterward, he has succeeded, down to this very day, and to a greater extent than has ever been the case elsewhere, in freeing all Mohammedan countries from those professional outcasts who live by their own misery, and, by their existence as a recognized class, are a standing reproach to every member of the society of which they form a part.

Mohammed did not abolish slavery altogether, for in that condition of society it would have been neither possible nor desirable to do so; but he encouraged the emancipation of slaves; he laid down the principle that every slave that embraced Islam should be *ipso facto* free, and, what is more important, he took care that no stigma should attach to the emancipated slave in consequence of his honest and honorable life of labor.   In Islam the emancipated slave is actually, as well as potentially, equal to a free-born citizen, and he often rises to one of the highest posts in the empire.†   As to those

---

* Sura vi., 138, 141, 152.

† Zeid, the freedman of the Prophet, often took the command in war. Captain Burton mentions ("Pilgrimage," vol. i., p. 89) that the pacha

who continued slaves, he prescribed kindness and con-
sideration in dealing with them.* "See," he said, in his
parting address at Mina, the year before his death—"see
that ye feed them with such food as ye eat yourselves,
and clothe them with the stuff ye yourselves wear; for
they are the servants of the Lord, and are not to be tor-
mented." The equality of all men before God was a
principle which Mohammed every where maintained;
and which, taking, as it did, all caste feeling from slavery, took away also its chief sting. To Mohammed's
mind labor could never be degrading, and the domestic
slavery of the Arabs, under which, thanks to him, parents were never to be separated from their children, nor
indeed relations from each other at all, though always
to be condemned in the abstract, became, under the
Prophet's hands, a bond closer and more lasting, and
hardly more liable to abuse, than domestic service elsewhere.

The orphan, too, is the subject of his peculiar care,
for he had been an orphan himself; and what God

---

of the Syrian caravan with which he traveled to Damascus had been the
slave of a slave. Sebuktegin, the father of the magnificent Mahmoud,
and founder of the Ghaznevide dynasty, was a slave; so was Kutb-ud-din,
the conqueror and first king of Delhi, and the true founder, therefore, of
the Mohammedan Empire in India. (See Elphinstone's "India," p. 320,
363, 370.)

* Sura xxiv., 34, 57.

had done for him, he was anxious, as far as might be, to do for others.* The poor were always present with him, and their condition never absent from his mind. In one of his early Suras, " the steep," as he calls it— that is to say, the straight and narrow way—is said to be to release the captive, to give food to the poor that lieth in the dust, and to stir up one another to steadfastness and compassion.† And in another Sura, Jews and Arabs are alike warned in their exclusive pride in their common progenitor, Abraham, that verily the nearest of kin to Abraham are they who follow him in his works.‡

Nor does Mohammed omit to lay stress on what I venture to think is as crucial a test of a moral code, and even of a religion, as is the treatment of the poor and the weak—I mean the duties we owe to what we call the lower animals. There is no religion which has taken a higher view of animal life in its authoritative documents, and none wherein the precept has been so much honored by its practical observance. " There is no beast on earth," says the Koran,§ " nor bird which flieth with its wings, but the same is a people like unto you—unto the Lord shall they return ;" and it is the current belief that animals will share with men the

---

* Sura viii., 42, and xciii., 6, to end.
† Sura xc., 12, 15, and *passim.*
‡ Sura iii., 61.                    § Sura vi., 38, and Sale's note *ad loc.*

general resurrection, and be judged according to their
works.  At the slaughter of an animal, the Prophet
ordered that God should always be named, but the
words " the Compassionate, the Merciful," were to be
omitted; for on the one hand such an expression
seemed a mockery to the sufferer, and, on the other,
he could not bring himself to believe that the destruction of any life, however necessary, could be altogether pleasing to the All Merciful.  " In the name of
God," says a pious Mussulman, before he strikes the
fatal blow—"God is most great; God give thee patience
to endure the affliction which he hath allotted thee!"*
In the East there has been no moralist like Bentham to
insist in noble words on the extension of the sphere of
morality to all sentient beings, and to be ridiculed for it
by people who call themselves religious; there has been
no naturalist like Darwin to demonstrate by his marvelous powers of observation how large a part of the mental and moral faculties which we usually claim for ourselves alone we share with other beings; there has been
no Oriental " Society for the Prevention of Cruelty to
Animals;" but one reason of this is not far to seek.
What the legislation of the last few years has at length
attempted to do, and, from the mere fact that it is legis-

---

* Lane's " Modern Egyptians," vol. i., p. 119.

lation, must do ineffectually, has been long effected in
the East by the moral and religious sentiment which,
like almost every thing that is good in that part of the
world, can be traced back, in part at least, to the great
Prophet of Arabia.*    In the East, so far as it has not
been hardened by the West, there is a real sympathy
between man and the domestic animals; they understand one another, and the cruelties which the most
humane of our countrymen unconsciously inflict in
the habitual use, for instance, of the muzzle or the
bearing-rein on the most docile, the most patient, the
most faithful, and the most intelligent of their companions, are impossible in the East. An Arab *can
not* ill-treat his horse; and Lane bears emphatic testimony to the fact that in his long residence in Egypt
he never saw an ass or a dog (though the latter is
there looked upon as an unclean animal) treated with

---

* The sympathy of the Prophet for his domestic animals is well known.
There is a great variety of traditions respecting his horses, his mules, his
milch and riding camels, and his goats.  It would be easy to write a complete biography of his favorite she-camel, Al Kaswa.  Her eccentricities
and perversities exercised an influence on some critical occasions in the
Prophet's life—*e. g.*, on his entrance to Medina, and at Kodeiba.  Among
the phenomena attending Mohammed's fits, it is recorded that if one came
on him while riding, his camel itself became first wildly excited, and then
fixed and rigid!  And I have little doubt that the story arose from the
almost electric sympathy that exists between an intelligent animal that is
kindly treated and its master.

cruelty, except in those cities which were overrun by Europeans.*

By absolutely prohibiting gambling and intoxicating liquors, Mohammed did much to abolish, once and for all, over the vast regions that own his sway, two of the worst and most irremediable evils of European society : evils to the intensity of which the Christian governments of the nineteenth century are hardly yet beginning to awake.† Can any one then deny what I have already hinted above, that, looking at him merely as a moral reformer, and apart from his great religious revolution, Mohammed was really doing Christ's work, even if he had reverenced Christ less than in fact he did ?

And this brings me to the most important question that I shall touch upon in this Lecture; and one but for which, in its various bearings, I do not know that I should have written these Lectures: I mean the attitude that Christianity ought to bear to Mohammedanism now. To say that in spite of the theoretic intolerance of Mohammedanism, it ought, unless its theory is put into practice, itself to be tolerated, is happily now a mere truism. But it ought not to be treated with a merely contemptuous or distant recognition, or to be inserted *tanquam infamiæ causâ*—" Jews, Turks, Infidels, and

---

* Lane, vol. i., p. 359–361.          † Sura v., 92.

Heretics"—in a collect, once a year, upon that day of all others upon which the universality of Christ's self-sacrifice is brought before us. When the draft of a treaty was brought to the General of the armies of revolutionary France, the first clause of which contained a formal recognition by the Emperor Francis of Austria—the representative of legitimacy, absolutism, and divine right—of the existence of the French Republic, "Strike that clause out," said Napoleon; "the French Republic needs no recognition from him—it is as clear as the sun at noonday." Mohammedanism needs no formal recognition of its existence by a faith with which it has so much in common. The immemorial quarrel between Mohammedanism and Christianity is, after all, a quarrel between near relations; and, like most immemorial quarrels, is based chiefly on mutual misunderstandings. Without any appearance of extraordinary condescension, we should recognize the fact which Mohammedans themselves might at present certainly be inclined to deny, that Islam is the nearest approach to Christianity—I would almost call it, remembering Mohammed's intense reverence for Christ, the only form of Christianity—which has proved itself suited to the nations of the East. Even Dante placed Mohammed in the "Inferno," not as a heathen, but as a heretic; and is there any reason who our notion of Christianity should be less comprehensive than his?

Mohammedanism is the one religion in the world, besides our own and the Jewish, which is strictly and avowedly Monotheistic. "Dispute not," said Mohammed to his followers, "against those who have received the Scriptures, that is, Jews and Christians, except with gentleness; but say unto them we believe in the revelation which hath been sent down to us, and also in that which hath been sent down to you; and our God and your God is one."* And again he says in another place, "Verily the Believers, and those who are Jews, those who are Christians and Sabeans, whoever believeth in God, and the last day, and doeth that which is right, they shall have their reward with their Lord—there shall come no fear upon them, neither shall they be grieved."† The three creeds are branches from the same parent stock, not different stocks; and they all alike look back to the majestic character of Abraham

---

* Sura v., 73.

† Sura ii., 59. There is a still more striking passage in v., 52–53: "Unto every one have we given a law and a way. Now if God had pleased, he would surely have made you one people, but he hath made you to differ that he might try you in that which he hath given to each, therefore strive to excel each other in good works. Unto God shall ye all return, and he will tell you that concerning which ye have disagreed."—Cf. Acts x., 35. These are passages on which the comparative mythologist, the Mussulman reformer, and the Christian missionary would alike do well to dwell. It is noteworthy also that the fifth Sura, from which two of them come, is placed by Rodwell and others last in the chronological order.

as the first teacher of the unity of God. Mohammed says, again and again, that the belief he inculcates is no new belief—it is the original creed of El-Khalil Allah, the Friend of God. The heroes of the Old Testament history, Isaac and Jacob, Joseph and Joshua, David and Solomon, are heroes of the Mohammedan religion as well as of the Jewish and Christian.

I remarked in my second Lecture that Mohammed may have thought himself justified in breaking the moral law he himself imposed, because a somewhat similar concession had been made to Moses. This is not a mere conjecture on my part, for it is certain that Mohammed had, for one who was so careless of facts, acquired somehow a full and fairly accurate knowledge of the history of the great Lawgiver. He relates it at length,* and recurs to it with a passionate fondness from an early period in his career, evidently dwelling mentally on the striking parallels between himself and Moses, the shepherd life, the call to the Prophet's office, the rejection by their own countrymen, no less than—be it always remembered to Mohammed's credit that he does not disguise it — the main point of difference, the prodigality of miracles performed by the one, and the inability to work them in the other. One most sa-

---

* See especially Suras vii., xviii., xxvii., xxviii., lv.

cred spot actually connects the two Prophets together.
There is a tradition, to some extent authenticated, that
Mohammed drove the camels of Kadijah to the very
place where Moses had tended the flocks of Jethro.
Moses and Mohammed may have reposed on the same
rock, watered their cattle at the same springs, looked
upon the same weird mountains.* And it is a redeeming point, perhaps the only redeeming point, in the
melancholy history of St. Catharine's Monastery, that
from age to age, within the convent walls, mosque and
church have stood side by side, and Mussulmans and
Christians have knelt together worshiping the same
God; and there, if only there in the world, venerating
with a kindred, if not with an equal reverence, the
same prophets, Moses and Mohammed, and One who
is infinitely greater than them both.†

Again, Mohammedanism is essentially a spiritual religion. As instituted by Mohammed it had "no priest
and no sacrifice;"‡ in other words, no caste of sacri-

---

* Sura ii., 57; vii., 160.

† See the account of St. Catharine's and its degradation in "The Desert of the Exodus," by E. H. Palmer; and in Stanley's "Sinai and Palestine," p. 53, 54. It is said that at Nijni Novgorod the same phenomenon, mosque and church as near and not unfriendly neighbors, may be
observed; but there no doubt it is commerce rather than religious sympathy which we have to thank for it.

‡ The sacrifice at the Annual Pilgrimage is a mere relic of the Pagan
practice; it has little religious significance, and does not imply priest-

ficing priests were ever to be allowed to come between the human soul and God: forbidding the representation of all living things alike, whether as objects of use or of admiration, of veneration or of worship, Mohammedanism is more opposed to idolatry even than we are ourselves. Mohammed hated images more sternly even than the Iconoclasts of Constantinople or the soldiers of Cromwell. Every mosque in the world of Islam bears witness to this. Statuary and pictures being forbidden, variegated marbles, and festoons of lamps, and geometric shapes, and tortuous inscriptions from the Koran have to supply their place as best they can, and form that peculiar species of ornamentation, strictly confined to the inanimate world, which we call Arabesque; and which is still to be traced in the architecture of so many churches and so many mosques along the frontier line of four thousand miles which divides the realm of the Crescent from that of the Cross.*

---

craft; it indicates only the belief that sin deserves death. In orthodox Mohammedanism there is no priestly caste, and therefore no fictions of apostolical succession, inherent sanctity, indissoluble vows, or powers of absolution. See Palgrave's "Essays," p. 82.

\* Cf. Stanley's "Lectures on the Eastern Church," p. 273. Without discussing the general question at length, I may remark here that Gothic architecture, though it is not very ready to acknowledge the debt, owes much to Moorish architecture—in particular the Horse-shoe or Crescent Arch. The pointed arch itself is to be found in many early mosques, and some of the most famous Venetian buildings, St. Mark's among them, owe much to Saracenic architecture.

This hatred of idolatry has been found even among the most uncivilized followers of the Prophet. The gorgeous ritual, the gaudy pictures, and the pious frauds which play so large a part in the conversion of the Sclavonian nations to Christianity seem only to have alienated these semi-barbarians. Mahmoud, the Ghaznevide, the son of a slave and the conqueror of Hindoostan, was offered a sum of ten millions sterling if only he would spare the famous idol in the pagoda of Somnat. Avarice is said to have been his besetting fault, but he replied in the memorable words, "Never shall Mahmoud be handed down to posterity as an idol seller, rather than an idol destroyer;" and broke it into pieces.*

Finally: Mohammedanism, in spite of centuries of wars and misunderstandings, looks back upon the Founder of our religion with reverence only less than that with which the most devout Christians regard him.

So far from its being true, as is commonly supposed, that Mohammedans regard Christ as Christians have too often regarded Mohammed, with hatred and with contempt, Sir William Muir remarks that devout Mussulmans never mention the name of Seyyedna Eesa, or

---

* Ferishta's "History of Mohammedan Power in India" (Briggs's translation), vol. i., p. 72 ; and Elphinstone's "History of India," p. 336.

Our Lord Jesus, without adding the words " on whom be peace."   The highest honor that a Mussulman can conceive is given to Christ in the grave reserved for him by the side of the Prophet himself in the great mosque at Medina.   Mohammedans expect that he will one day return to earth, and having slain Antichrist, will establish perfect peace among men.   And Mr. Hunter* tells us that the Indian Sheeahs avowedly look forward to his reappearance simultaneously with that of the last of their twelve Imams, and to an amalgamation of the two creeds: of Islam as the followers of Ali hold it, and of Christianity, not as it is, but as they believe it was taught by Christ himself.†

If it be asked, why then did Mohammed not accept Christianity, I apprehend that the reasons are threefold; and that it appears, from the chronological order lately assigned to the Suras of the Koran, that at one period, that of the Fatrah, Mohammed did consider whether first Judaism, and secondly Christianity, as he knew it, contained the message he had to give.

I. The first explanation I would suggest is, that the Christ known to him was the Christ, not of the Bible,

* "Our Indian Mussulmans," p. 120, by W.W. Hunter.

† For a curious discussion on the return of the Messiah to earth held at Timbuctoo, see Barth's "Travels in Central Africa," vol. v., p. 4.

but of tradition; the Christ, not of the Canonical, but
of the Apocryphal Gospels, and even these only from
general tradition.  The wonder is, Mohammed's information being confined to the incoherent rhapsodies and
the miraculous inanities of the Gospels of the Infancy,
the Acta Pilati and the "Descensus ad Inferos," not
that he reverenced Christ so little, but so much.  In the
whole of the Koran there are only three passages which
look like any direct acquaintance with the Evangel-
ists; and one of these, the well-known passage about
the Paraclete, he misunderstands himself, and accuses
Christians of intentionally perverting from its proper
meaning a prediction of the coming of the Periclyte,
the Greek form of Mohammed, the Illustrious, or the
Praised.*

II. Secondly, the worship of saints and images, and
the shape which certain floating ideas had taken when
they were stereotyped in the formulas of the Christian
Church, seemed to Mohammed to conflict with his fundamental doctrine of the unity of God.  The mysteries
of the Trinity were to be appraised and handled by
every one who called himself a Christian, not merely as
a test, but as the test of his Christianity.  Mohammed
accuses even the Jews of having lost sight of their pri-

---

* Sura lxi., 6.

mary truth, which was also his, in calling Ezra the Son
of God;* and what wonder if he rejected a religion the
essence of which he understood, and too many Christians of his time understood, to be, not a holy life, but,'
as it is still represented in the Athanasian Creed, an
elaborate and unthinkable mode of thinking of the
Trinity?†

Let us hear on these points Mohammed himself, remembering all the while how slight was his knowledge
of the doctrine which he travestied, and how dim the
outline of the majestic character which yet filled his
imagination:

"They surely are infidels who say God is the third of
three, for there is no god but one God."‡

"Say not three; forbear, it will be better for thee;
God is only one God."§

Christ was with Mohammed the greatest of Prophets.‖ He had the power of working miracles; he spoke

---

* Sura ix., 30.

† It is doubtful whether a people that has once become monotheistic in
any other form than the Christian can ever be brought to accept, I do
not say Christianity altogether, but the doctrines that are often supposed
to be of its very essence. Among such a people the missionary invariably
finds that the doctrine of the Trinity, however explained, involves Trithe-
ism, and their ears are at once closed to his teaching. To a Pagan who
accepts Christianity the change no doubt is one from Polytheism to Monotheism, but to the Jew or Mohammedan, except in very rare instances,
it is the opposite.

‡ Sura v., 77.　　§ Sura iv., 6.　　‖ Sura ii., 254.

in his cradle; he made a bird out of clay. (Incidents drawn from the Gospels of the Infancy or of St. Thomas.) He could give sight to the blind, and even raise the dead to life.* He is the Word proceeding from God; his name is the Messiah. Illustrious in this world and in the next, and one of those who have near access to God.† "He is strengthened by the Holy Spirit," for so Mohammed, in more than one passage, calls the Angel Gabriel.‡ Mohammed all but believes in the Immaculate Conception of the Virgin,§ and certainly in the miraculous nature of the birth of Christ, to which he recurs repeatedly.|| But that Jesus ever claimed, as is affirmed by the writers of the New Testament, and as we know he did, to be the Son of God, still less that he ever claimed to be equal with God, Mohammed could not bring himself to believe.

"It becometh not a man that God should give him the Scriptures, and the Wisdom, and the spirit of Prophecy, and that then he should say to his followers, Be ye worshipers of me as well as of God; but rather, Be

---

* Sura iii., 41–43.          † Sura iii., 40.          ‡ Sura ii., 81.

§ Sura iii., 30. There was a well-known sect of Christians called Collyridians in Arabia who paid the Virgin divine honors, and offered her a twisted cake (κόλλυρις). Thence, no doubt, came Mohammed's idea that the Virgin was one of the Persons of the Trinity.

|| Sura xix., 20.

ye perfect in things pertaining to God, since ye know the Scriptures, and have studied them."*

And again, " For the Messiah himself said, O children of Israel, worship God, my Lord and yours."†

And once more, "Those who say that Jesus, the Son of Mary, is the Son of God, are infidels, for who could stop the arm of God if he were to destroy the Messiah and his mother, and all who are in the earth together?"‡

Neither can Mohammed ever believe that Jesus could have been crucified. " It is so long ago, let us hope that it is not true," said an old Cumberland woman when she heard for the first time in her life the story of the Crucifixion. " If I and my brave Franks had been there, we would have avenged his injuries," was the exclamation of the fierce barbarian Clovis when he received his first lesson in the Christian life. The Dreamer of the Desert sympathized rather with the first of these. As Stesichorus§ believed that the Greeks and Trojans fought for the phantom of Helen, and not for Helen herself; as the Docetists held that the phantom of Jesus and not Jesus had been crucified; so Mohammed rebels at the thought that God can ever have allowed such a tragedy to take place. Some one else, he curiously supposes, who deserved such a death—perhaps

---

* Sura iii., 73.

† Sura v., 76.

‡ Sura v., 19.

§ Plato, " Republic," ix., 386.

it was Judas himself—may have been substituted for Christ; and Christ being taken up to heaven, must have felt that the deception thus practiced on the Jews was a kind of punishment to himself for not having taken greater pains to prevent men calling him the Son of God.* And at the resurrection Jesus will himself testify against both Jews and Christians; the Jews for not having received him as a prophet, the Christians for having received him as God.

There is a short chapter in the Koran which Mussulmans look upon as equal to a third of the whole in value:

> "Say there is one God alone—
> God the Eternal;
> He begetteth not, and he is not begotten,
> And there is none like unto him."†

And once more, "They say the Merciful hath gotten offspring. Now have ye done a monstrous thing; almost might the very heavens rend thereat, and the earth rend asunder, and the mountains fall down in fragments, that they ascribe a son to the Merciful, when it becometh not the Merciful to beget a son. Verily there is nobody in the heavens nor in the earth that shall approach the Merciful but as a servant."‡

I have dwelt thus at length upon Mohammed's views

---

* Sura iii., 49; iv., 156.    † Sura cxii.    ‡ Sura xix., 91–94.

of Christ, partly because of the intrinsic interest and importance attaching to the views held by one so great of one so infinitely greater; partly because they show how little Mohammed, and indeed how little Christians themselves, understood the real nature of Christianity; partly also because the strictures of Mohammed, however exaggerated and however mistaken, seem to me to suggest a caution necessary for us all. Christ came to reveal God, not to hide him; to bring him down to earth, not to shroud him in an immeasurable distance; to tell us that God is not primarily Justice, or Truth, or Power, but Love. Do Christians always remember this? Are our views of Justification, of Original Sin, of a Future Life, when drawn out in the forensic and almost legal language in which some churches foolishly delight to clothe them, always consistent with it? Do our prayers always pre-suppose a God who, in his own intrinsic nature, is anxious to receive them? Are we not apt to forget the unity of God while we dogmatize on the Trinity? Do we not sometimes place Christ, as it were, in front of God, thinking so much of the Son who sacrificed himself that we ignore the Father who "spared him not"—forgetting the Giver in the very magnitude of the gift?

III. And the third reason, and perhaps the most important of all, for Mohammed's rejection of Christianity,

is the fact that Christianity as he knew it had been tried
and had failed. It had been known for three hundred
years in Arabia, and had not been able to overthrow, or
even weaken, the idolatry of the inhabitants.

It is strange, with this fact and the whole course of
history before him, with which evidently few are more
familiar, that a great writer can conclude a review of
Mohammedanism, which is otherwise fair and able, by
indorsing the charge made against it that it has kept
back the East by hindering the spread of Christianity.
The charge has been often made before,* but it rests
on so slender a basis that I should not have thought
it necessary to discuss it here had I not found at the
last moment that one who is apparently so high an
authority has lent the weight of his name to it. That
I may do him no injustice, I quote his own words:

"Mohammed in his own age and country was the
greatest of reformers—a reformer alike religious, moral,
and political. . . . But when his system passed the borders of the land in which it was so great a reform, it
became the greatest of curses to mankind. The main
cause which has made the religion of Mohammed exercise so blighting an influence on every land where it
has been preached, is because it is an imperfect system

---

* As, for instance, by Sir W. Muir, vol. iv., p. 321.

standing in the way of one more perfect.  Islam has in
it just enough of good to hinder the reception of greater
good. . . . Because Islam comes nearer to Christianity
than any other false system, because it comes nearer
than any other to satisfying the wants of man's spiritual
nature, for that very reason it is, above all other false
systems, pre-eminently anti-Christian.  It is, as it were,
the personal enemy and rival of the Faith, disputing on
equal terms for the same prize!" *

This indictment is so well drawn, at first sight it so
carries conviction with it, and yet, if true, it is so fatal
to any favorable or any fair judgment of Mohammedanism, that I am compelled, while I gladly acknowledge
the author's fair and sympathetic treatment of the subject in every page that precedes and follows those I have
quoted, to contest, from my point of view, as strongly as
I can, upon this question, alike his facts and his inferences.

Upon what single fact, then, either before or after
Mohammed's time, does the writer ground this charge?
If the purest Christianity of all, preached by Christ and
his Apostles, did not make way in the Eastern world;
if the few Christian churches which did exist among
the half Roman or Hellenic inhabitants of Syria and of

Africa had sunk to the condition in which we know they were when Mohammedanism swept them away, what reason have we, either *à priori* or *à posteriori*, for supposing that the Christianity of any later time would have been more successful? Have Christian nations been so energetic or so successful in converting any of those African or Asiatic nations which Mohammedanism has never reached, as to entitle us to turn round upon the religion which has remoulded so large a portion of the human race, and tell it that it is a curse to humanity because, forsooth, while we admit it was in its time a grand forward movement and has been a higher life to untold millions since, we wish that Fetich worship should have lasted on perhaps till now, that Christianity may now have the chance of doing the work somewhat better? If this is Christianity, I only say most certainly it is not of Christ. It is not of the spirit of him who said that those who were not against him were with him; and rejoiced that good was done by others, even if it seemed an infringement of his own divine commission. Christ was not like the Prætorian prefect of Tacitus, "*Consilii, quamvis egregii, quod non ipse afferret inimicus,*" though some Christians would have it that he was. The only monopoly of good that Christianity, if it is of the spirit of its Founder, may claim, is the monopoly, not of doing good, but of rejoicing at it whenever it is done, and whoever does it; of showing, if it carries out its Founder's intentions, that it is wide enough to recognize as its own and to embrace within its ample bosom all honest "seekers after God," and all true benefactors of humanity. The most "anti-Christian" religion is not that which comes nearest to Christianity, but that which is furthest removed from it; and the religion which after Christianity comes nearest to "satisfying the wants of man's spiritual nature" is really not its most deadly enemy, but its best ally. To say otherwise, liberal and tolerant as the author unquestionably is, is to encourage weaker men under the shadow of his name,* not merely to indulge in the *odium theologicum*, but to assert that the *odium theologicum* itself is Christian.

> "Non tali auxilio nec defensoribus istis
> Tempus eget."

Can it be forgotten that the churches planted by the great Apostle were, without exception, to the west of Palestine—that star-worship and fire-worship were unaffected by Christianity then, even as Brahminism and Buddhism are unaffected by it now? Can we point to a

---

* This has actually been the case, for the passage I have quoted was the only one in an otherwise most temperate essay upon which religious periodicals pounced, and, by quoting apart from its context, fanned the flame of misconception and prejudice which, even when read with every thing which tends the other way, it would, in my judgment, be likely to kindle.

single Oriental nation which has been able to accept and to retain Christianity in its pure form, or to a single religion to be named with Mohammedanism in point of purity and sublimity, which has ever been able to overthrow any national Oriental faith? And, if we can not, what right have we to say that it is Islam, and not Nature, that has hitherto stood in the way of Christianity in Arabia and Persia, in Africa and India? The triumphs of the Cross have indeed been far purer, far wider, far sublimer than those of the Crescent; but they have been hitherto confined to the higher races of the world. Uncivilized nations of the higher stock—Ostrogoths and Visigoths, Vandals and Lombards, Franks and Northmen, the Celt, the Teuton, and the Sclavonian—invaded Christianity only to be conquered by it. But upon the Oriental barbarians of a lower race who invaded Europe, with the one exception of the Magyars, whose case is special *—Huns and Avars, Turks and Tartars—it has

---

* The Magyars, whatever their original home—and it seems that they were of the Finnish stock—are probably the most mixed race on the Continent of Europe, and were so even before they settled within the limits of the present Hungary. In their march toward Europe they were joined by hosts of Chazars, Bulgarians, and Sclavonians. During their ravages, which lasted for some fifty years, and spread from the Oural Mountains to the Pyrenees, they transported women and children wholesale from the countries they overran to their head-quarters on the Danube; and it is probable that at the time of their avowed conversion by Adalbert, about A.D. 1000, they had at least as much German and Italian as they had Tartar blood in their veins. St. Piligrinus (quoted by Gibbon,

had no influence. Shall Christians, then, complain of Mohammedans for having succeeded in some measure in doing for the East what they have failed to do; or would Christ have rejected what good service Mohammed did because his credentials were not precisely those of the Apostles? What superficial appearance of truth there is in the charge is this—that no Mohammedan nation has hitherto accepted Christianity, while some nations that were nominally Christians have accepted Mohammedanism. But to establish the charge it would, of course, be necessary to show that the East, if it had not accepted Mohammedanism, would have accepted a real Christianity, or any religion so much like Christianity as Mohammedanism unquestionably is; and to do this we must read history backward.

Now Mohammed offered to the Arabs an idea of God less sympathetic and less lovable, indeed, but as sublime as the Christian, and perhaps still more intense, and one, as it turned out, which they could receive. Christianity was compelled to leave its birthplace—the inhabitants and subsequent history of which it has scarcely affected, except indirectly—to find its proper home in the Western world, among the inhabitants and progressive civil-

---

vol. vii., p. 172), the first missionary who entered Hungary, says that he found the "majority of the population to be Christians," *qui ex omni parte mundi illuc tracti sunt captivi.*

ization of Greece and Rome. The lot of Mohammedanism has been different; "it is the religion of the shepherd and the nomad, of the burning desert and the boundless steppe." So admirably suited was it to the region in which it was born, that it needed no foreign air or change of circumstances to develop it.[*]

In its simple grandeur it has been able, without tampering with that which is its Alpha and Omega—the belief in one God, who reveals himself by his prophets —to leave the most essential elements of national life to the various nations which made up the Arabian Empire; and to adapt itself to every peculiarity, mental and moral, of the inhabitants of Central and Western Asia. The rapid intuition and the wild flights of imagination; the vivid mental play around the antinomies of the reason, and the craving for the supernatural in the utmost particularity of detail; the fervid asceticism of the Dervish, and the mystic Pantheism of the Soufy, have each found in Islam something to meet their wants.

But, on the other hand, Mohammedanism has never passed into countries of a wholly different nature, and held them permanently. Spain is not a case in point, though it was never so well governed as under the Mohammedans; for the Spaniards themselves never became

---

[*] Compare throughout this paragraph, M. Barthélemy St. Hilaire, p. 230, seq.

Mohammedan, and the Moorish settlement there was only like a Greek ἐπιτείχισμα or a Roman colonia—an outpost in the heart of the enemy's country. Much the same may be said of Turkey, where the subject population has always remained Christian. I can not, therefore, "*pace tanti nominis,*" follow Gibbon in his picture of the probable consequences to European civilization had Charles Martel been conquered at Tours—of Mussulman preachers demonstrating to a circumcised audience, in the mosques of Paris and of Oxford, the truth of the religion of Mohammed! The wave of conquest might have spread over Europe; but it would have been but a wave, and few traces would have been left when it had swept on. In Africa the case was different; the Greek colonists and Roman conquerors—the higher races, in fact—were driven out by the Saracens, and, "in their climate and habits, the wandering Moors who remained behind already resembled the Bedouins of the desert." * Mohammedanism is the only form in which the knowledge of the true God has ever made way with the native races of Africa; and the form of Christianity which it supplanted in the North—the Christianity of the Donatists and of the Nitrian monks; of Cyril, strangely called a saint; and of the infamous George of

* Gibbon, vol. vi., p. 473.

Cappadocia, still more strangely transformed into St. George of England, the patron of chivalry and of the Garter—was infinitely inferior to Mohammedanism itself.

I fully admit that Mohammedanism, if indeed it had succeeded in conquering the most civilized races of the world and the Christianity of the West, as it succeeded in conquering the Eastern nations and their various forms of belief, would have conquered something that was potentially better than itself, and then it would have been what Christian writers are so fond of calling it— a curse to the world rather than a blessing. It would have stepped beyond what I conceive to have been its proper mission; but I maintain that it stopped short of this, and that it destroyed nothing that was not far inferior to itself. I should hesitate to say that even its conquest of Spain was not, while it lasted, a blessing to Spain itself, and through Spain to the whole of Europe. Has Spain exhibited more order, more toleration, more industry, better faith, more material prosperity, under her most Christian Kings or under her Ommiade Kaliphs? The names of the three Abdal Rahmans, and of Almamun, suggest all that is most glorious in Spanish history, and much that has conferred benefit on the rest of Europe in the darkest period of her annals—religious zeal without religious intolerance, philosophy and litera-

ture, science and art, hospitals and libraries and univer-
sities.

It follows, from what I have said, that Mohammedanism is not a world-wide religion. The sphere of its influence is vast, but not boundless; in catholicity of application it is as much below the purest Christianity as
the Semitic and Turanian nations which have embraced
it are below the Western Indo-Germanic. I say the
Western Indo-Germanic races, for among the Eastern
branches of that great family, the inhabitants of Persia and of Hindoostan, Mohammedanism did establish
itself.

The Persians are of a race and genius widely different
from the Arabs; but the surroundings and the general
mode of life are the same in each, and the exception, so
far as it is an exception, to the rule I have laid down,
tends rather, in its results, to prove its general truth, for
the hold of Mohammedanism on them has been much
modified by the difference of race. The religion which
proclaimed the absolute supremacy of God was no doubt
an infinite advance upon the " chilling equipoise " of
good and evil to which the creed of Zoroaster had at
that time sunk.* Nor was the national existence of
Persia stamped out, as has been often said, by the Ka-

* See Elphinstone's " India," vol. v., p. 313.

liphs; for the Persian province of Khorasan was itself strong enough to place the Abbasside Kaliphs on the throne of Bagdad; and the Persian dynasties of the Samanides and Dilemites gave to the nation a new lease of life, and a wholly new national literature; and it is to a Mohammedan Sultan of the Turkish race that Persia owes her greatest literary glory, her national epic, the "Shahnameh" of Ferdousi. Still it can not be said that the religion proved itself altogether suited to the people. In other countries the scimiter had no sooner been drawn from its scabbard than it was sheathed again. But in Persia the scimiter had not only to clear the way, but for some time afterward to maintain the new religion.* The Persians corrupted its simplicity with fables and with miracles; they actually imported into it something of saint-worship and something of sacerdotalism; and, consequently, in no nation in the Mohammedan world has the religion less hold on the people as a restraining power. The most stringent principles of the Koran are set at naught; beng and opium are common; the Ketman, or religious equivocation, is held to be as allowable as it has been by the Casuists or the Jesuits; and the nation which Herodotus tells us devoted a third of its whole educational curriculum to learning to speak

---

* See Sir John Malcolm's "History of Persia," vol. i., p. 277, etc.

the truth, now contains hardly an individual who will speak the truth unless he has something to gain by it.

In Hindoostan, amid the other branch of the great Aryan race which did not move westward, Mohammedanism has obtained finally a very strong footing; but it was slow in winning its way; and the thirty million Mussulmans over whom we rule — and a tremendous and but half-recognized responsibility it is* — devout as they are, have become so by long lapse of time, by social influences, and by intermixture with conquering Arabs, Ghaznevides, and Affghans, rather than by the sudden fervor of religious enthusiasm.†

Those who have followed me thus far will perceive that my main object in writing these Lectures has been, if possible, to render some measure of that justice to Mohammed and to his religion which has been all too long, and is still all too generally, denied to them. I have naturally, therefore, been led to dwell rather on the points in which Mohammedanism resembles Christianity than on the points in which it differs, and I have been led, also, to some extent, to compare the per-

---

* Since this was written the grievances of Mohammedans in India, so ably and temperately stated by Mr. Hunter, have been in part alleviated by the adoption of some of the remedies he suggests, at least as far as regards education.

† Elphinstone, vol. v., p. 314, and cap. iii. on the reign of the Sultan Mahmoud.

sons of their respective Founders. It is not possible to avoid this. Of the Founder of Christianity I have necessarily spoken only under that aspect of his character which Mussulman as well as Christian, friend as well as foe, will perforce allow him; and in which alone, by the nature of the case, he can be compared with any other founder at all. In like manner, in comparing the two creeds, I have insisted mainly on the points in which they approximate to each other; and to do this is more necessary, more just, and, I venture to think, more Christian, than to do the opposite.

But if, in order to prevent misconception, the two creeds must necessarily be contrasted rather than compared, nothing that I have said, or am going to say, will prevent my admitting fully—what, indeed, is apparent upon the face of it—that the contrasts are at least as striking as the resemblances.

The religion of Christ contains whole fields of morality and whole realms of thought which are all but outside the religion of Mohammed. It opens humility, purity of heart, forgiveness of injuries, sacrifice of self to man's moral nature; it gives scope for toleration, development, boundless progress to his mind; its motive power is stronger, even as a friend is better than a king, and love higher than obedience. Its realized ideals in the various paths of human greatness have been more com-

manding, more many-sided, more holy, as Averroes is
below Newton, Haroun below Alfred, and Ali below
St. Paul. Finally, the ideal life of all is far more elevating, far more majestic, far more inspiring, even as
the life of the founder of Mohammedanism is below
the life of the Founder of Christianity.

And when I speak of the ideal life of Mohammedanism I must not be misunderstood. There is in Mohammedanism no ideal life in the true sense of the word,
for Mohammed's character was admitted by himself to
be a weak and erring one. It was disfigured by at least
one huge moral blemish; and exactly in so far as his
life has, in spite of his earnest and reiterated protesta-
tions, been made an example to be followed, has that
vice been perpetuated. But in Christianity the case is
different. The words, "Which of you convinceth me
of sin?" forced from the mouth of Him who was meek
and lowly of heart, by the wickedness of those who,
priding themselves on being Abraham's children, never
did the works of Abraham, are a definite challenge to
the world. That challenge has been for nineteen centuries before the eyes of unfriendly, as well as of believing, readers, and it has never yet been fairly met;
and at this moment, by the confession of friend and foe
alike, the character of Jesus of Nazareth stands alone in
its spotless purity and its unapproachable majesty. We

have each of us probably at some period of our lives tried hard to penetrate to the inmost meaning of some one of Christ's short and weighty utterances—

> "Those jewels, five words long,
> Which on the stretched forefinger of all time
> Sparkle forever."

But is there one of us who can say there is no more behind ?   Is there one thoughtful person among us who has ever studied the character of Christ, and has not, in spite of ever-recurring difficulties and doubts, once and. again burst into the centurion's exclamation, "Truly this was the Son of God ?"

Nor are the methods of drawing near to God the same in the two religions. The Mussulman gains a knowledge of God—he can hardly be said to approach him—by listening to the lofty message of God's Prophet.   The Christian believes that he approaches God by a process which, however difficult it may be to define, yet has had a real meaning to Christ's servants, and has embodied itself in countless types of Christian character — that mysterious something which St. Paul calls a " union with Christ."   " Ye are dead, and your life is hid with Christ in God."

But this unmistakable superiority does not shake my position that Mohammedanism is, after all, an approach to Christianity, and perhaps the nearest approach

to it which the unprogressive part of humanity can
ever attain in masses; and yet how large a part of the
whole human race are unprogressive! Whatever we
may wish, and however current conversation and literature may assert the contrary, progress is the exception,
and not the rule, with mankind. The whole Eastern
world, with very few exceptions, has been hitherto and
is still stationary, not progressive. What Oriental society is now, it was in the time of Solomon—I might say,
in the time of Abraham. Even those nations which,
like the Chinese, have considerable powers of invention
and mechanical skill, reach a certain height rapidly, and
then stop short.*

Accepting, then, the non-progressiveness of a large
part of the human race, when left to themselves, as a
fact, can not we estimate other religions, not by our
conception of what we want, but by their bearing on
the life of those whom they affect, ennobling them so
far as the other conditions of their existence may ren-

---

* I specify China; for I can not accept the changes relied upon by Dr.
Bridges in his very able essay on China, in "International Policy," as
being evidence of continuous and progressive change, which is the real
point at issue. Of course this in no way affects the more important
questions treated of in the essay, the moral elevation of which seems to
me almost unequaled in the writings even of those who, like the contrib-
utors to the volume referred to, and the followers of Auguste Comte generally, have labored most earnestly to treat all political questions from a
moral stand-point.

der possible ? Judged by this relative standard—which is, as I conceive, the only true one—Mohammedanism has nothing to lose, and every thing to gain, by the keenest criticism.* I grant to the full every thing that can be said by travelers such as Burckhardt and Burton and Palgrave upon the degradation of the mass of the Bedouins and the Turks, and the want of all vital religion, sometimes of the very elements of religion, among them. But is the state of the Mohammedan world as a whole worse in proportion to its light than was that of Christendom when the cup of iniquity was full and a Luther was born ? To take a particular instance, has religion less hold upon the Arabs than it had upon the English throughout the last century, till the evangelical revival of Wesley and Whitefield aroused it from its sleep? Has it less hold even upon the " Frenchmen of the East," as the Persians have been called—liars, drunkards, profligate though they are—than it has at this moment upon the Frenchmen of the West? What account do travelers in Russia give us of the state of religion among the masses there? And what judgment

* Abyssinia is a case in point for those who think that a religion, because it is better and purer in itself, is necessarily better than all other religions, wherever and whenever and in whatever degree of purity it may be found. Abyssinia has been nominally Christian since very early times, and yet it would puzzle the greatest enemy of Islam to name a single particular in which the inhabitants are superior to their Mussulman neigh-

must pious Mohammedans form of Christianity, if their knowledge of it is confined to the average lives of Europeans who profess it?

To say that gross abuses have crept into Mohammedanism—that the lives of many, or even of the majority, who profess it are a disgrace to their name—is only to say that it is not exempt from the common conditions of humanity.

Take one instance, drawn from the history of the Christian Church. Christianity was in its origin and in its essence a creed entirely spiritual; but Christians, forming, as they did, a new human society, were allowed by their Founder to symbolize this close union, and to bring it home more vividly to themselves and to the world, by two external rites. The mere fact that they were external, in a religion which was otherwise a matter of the heart, ought to have put men on their guard, lest they should assume in time a too prominent place; lest what was accidental and secondary and relative should dominate over what was absolute and primary

---

bors. Spain may suggest similar thoughts. We are apt to forget that there are two factors to be considered in testing the value of a religion in any given case—the creed itself and the people who receive it. There are of course good and bad men, and these of every degree of goodness and badness, to be found professing every creed; but the average morality of the followers of an imperfect creed may, in this very imperfect world, be better than the average morality of those who profess a higher one, and of course *vice versa*. Πάντων μέτρον ἄνθρωπος.

and eternal. Baptism was of considerable importance in the infancy of the Church, for it was a pledge of fidelity consciously and voluntarily given by a new recruit, in the face of the enemy, to a cause whose victories were yet in the future. It was, as it were, the uniform assumed by the small army which at its Master's bidding went forth against the world. The love-feast also was of special importance among the earliest Christians, as a constant reminder that those who had taken upon themselves the commission of the Cross, that crowning act of love, were bound to one another by the same enthusiasm of love which bound them to their common Master. Both did good service then, and in the history of the Christian Church have done good service since, in so far as they have acted upon the heart, and thence upon the conduct, through the medium of a powerful appeal to the religious imagination. But in so far as any mysterious or supernatural efficacy has been attached to the form of either, they have sapped the root of Christianity. They have done for Christianity what of good, no doubt, Mohammed thought — and half rightly, half wrongly thought—that pilgrimages to the holy places might do for Mohammedanism. Both were so far concessions to human weakness that they introduced formal, or even material, conceptions into a spiritual religion; both, in fact, were capable of being used to advantage; and experience has proved that they were both alike liable to the same kind of abuse.

Every human institution, therefore—religion itself, so far as man can affect it—is exposed to inevitable decay; and the purer the religion, the more inevitable the degradation which contact with the world, which is not of it, must bring.[*] Accordingly, a religion which is not waiting for a revival, is waiting only till it be swept away.

But, on the other hand, we must not judge of a religion by its perversions or corruptions; and it is as fair to take Turkish despots and maniac dervishes and Persian libertines as types of the Mohammedan life, as it would be to take Anabaptists or Pillar Saints or Jesuits as types of the Christian life. Most of the well-known vices of our Mohammedan fellow-subjects in India are Indian vices, and not Mohammedan. Max Müller has remarked with truth, that without constant reformation —that is to say, without a constant return to the fountain-head—every religion, however pure, must gradually degenerate. Christianity has always reformed itself, and will to the end of time continue to reform itself, by going back to the words and to the life of Christ. It is a maxim of the Buddhists that "what has been said by Buddha, that alone is well said;"[†] and it is currently be-

---

[*] Max Müller, "Chips," Preface, p. 23.
[†] Quoted by Max Müller, loc. cit., p. 23.

lieved that Mohammedanism is dying out because it has
no such power of revival.   But the very reverse of this
is, rather, true.   Probably no religion has produced, in
the various parts of its vast empire, a more continuous
succession of reformers, whose aim has been to bring it
back to its original simplicity and purity.   Such was
one object, however wildly they set about it, of the Car-
mathians in the ninth century; and, to select one
among many individual reformers, such was the career
of Abdul Wahhab, the son of a petty Arabian sheik, a
hundred and fifty years ago.   The facts I take almost
*verbatim* from an interesting and able essay on "Our
Indian Mussulmans" by Dr. Hunter.*

Commencing by a moral attack upon the profligacy
of the Turkish pilgrims and the mummeries which pro-
faned the holy cities, Abdul Wahhab gradually elaborat-
ed a theological system which is substantially identical
with the original creed of Mohammed.   He taught, first,
absolute reliance on one God, and the rejection of all
mediators between man and God, whether saints or Mohammed himself; second, the right of private interpretation of the Koran; third, the prohibition of all forms
and ceremonies with which the pure faith has been over-
laid in the lapse of centuries; finally—and this is the

---

* See Hunter, p. 55–60; and for a further account of the Arab movement, see Burckhardt's "Notes on the Bedouins and Wahhabees."

only part to be regretted in the movement — he reasserted the obligation to wage war upon the infidel. In 1803 Wahhab's successors took the holy cities, and desecrated the sacred mosque at Mecca and the Prophet's tomb at Medina, to save them from the greater desecration, as it seemed to those Puritans of the Desert, involved in the almost divine honors lavished on them by ignorant or profligate pilgrims.

Here was an act upon the significance of which we may well dwell for a moment, and endeavor, by comparing it with somewhat parallel and better-known cases, to realize what it must have seemed like then, and what it proves about Mohammedanism now. Imagine the feelings of pious Jews when their most religious king broke into pieces the relic of relics, the memorial of the divine deliverance and of their desert life, and stigmatized it as a bit of brass! Imagine, if you can, the feelings of the Apostles when it dawned upon them that one of their number, even then, was a traitor in his heart! Imagine, to take a parallel case suggested by Mr. Hunter,[*] mediæval Christendom, when the news spread that Bourbon's cutthroats were installed in the Vatican, and that the head of the Christian Church had been taken captive by the Church's eldest son! Imagine Luther, when in the fervor of youthful enthusiasm he visited the Rome of

---

* Hunter, p. 59.

the Martyrs and of the Apostles, and found it to be the Rome of the Papacy, the Rome of impostures and indulgences, of the Borgias and the Medici! And we can then picture to ourselves the thrill of horror that must have passed through the orthodox Mussulman world when they heard that a sect of reformers, whose one idea of reform was a return to the life and doctrine of the Prophet, had rifled the mosque whose immemorial sanctity the Prophet had himself increased by making it the Kiblah of the world, and had even violated the Prophet's tomb. Imagine, on the other hand, what it must have cost the Wahhabees to have, like Luther, the courage of their convictions, to appear to stultify themselves, to dishonor their Prophet, and all that they might make their religion the spiritual religion that it had once been! And then say, if you can, that Mohammedanism has no power of self-reform, and is dying gradually of inanition!

Beaten down at last by the strong arm of Mehemet Ali, Pasha of Egypt, in 1812, helped, I regret to say, by Englishmen, the Wahhabees disappeared temporarily from Arabia,* only to reappear in 1821 in In-

---

* For a graphic and not very favorable account of the Wahhabee Empire, as it exists now in Arabia and its seat of government at Riad, see Palgrave's " Arabia," chap. ix.–xiii. There are one or two passages in this account, e. g., vol. i., p. 365–373, 427–437, in which I can not but think, with all my admiration for Mr. Palgrave's varied powers, that he has not been, even on his own showing elsewhere, altogether fair to Islam as a system.

dia, under the leadership of the prophet Sayyed Ah-
mad ; and the despised sect of Wahhabees are now,
perhaps, the real ruling spirit of Mussulman politics
in India, and enjoy the singular honor of having, as
much, no doubt, by their gloomy fanaticism as by their
moral lives and their missionary zeal, attracted to themselves considerable attention even from their English
rulers at home. Puritans of the Puritans of Islam,
they are despised and hated by the so-called orthodox
Mussulmans, as the Lutherans were hated by Leo, and
the Covenanters by Claverhouse.

The extraordinary phenomena attending the great
religious movement called Bâbyism now going on in
Persia, the ecstatic martyrdoms and the prodigality of
tortures submitted to amid songs of triumph by wom-
en and children, the followers of the " Bâb," are well
worth the study of all who are interested in the history of religion ; and, however we explain the facts,
much that I said of Wahhabeeism may, *mutatis mu-
tandis,* be said of it ; and at all events its existence
is a standing proof that Persian Mohammedanism
possesses so much of vitality as is necessary to adapt
an old creed to a new belief.*

When I first wrote the above paragraphs on the

* See Gobineau, "Les Religions et les Philosophies dans l'Asie Centrale," p. 141–215.

power of revival which I conceive to be inherent in Islam, I did not know that my words were at that very time being illustrated in the most striking way, not only in India and Persia and Arabia, upon which I then dwelt, but also throughout the Asiatic dominions of the Ottoman Sultans. Since then Mr. Palgrave's most interesting "Essays on Eastern Questions" have come into my hands; and I find in them both evidence to show that there is such a revival, and a graphic account of its leading symptoms.

Secular and denominational schools are every where giving place to schools of the most strictly Mussulman type. Mosques which were deserted are now crowded with worshipers; mosques which were in ruins are re-built. There is a general reaction, not perhaps to be wondered at, against the employment in public offices of the European and the Christian. Wine and spirit shops are closed, for their trade is gone except among the Levantine residents. Even opium and tobacco are becoming luxuries which are not only forbidden, but also forsaken.

Add to this, what Mr. Palgrave has also shown, that a new nation is as it were growing up under our eyes in Eastern Anatolia, rich with all the elements of a vigorous national and religious life, and we shall then have reason to believe that though the Ottoman supremacy

may pass away, as Kaliphs and Sultans, Attabeks and
Khans, Padishahs and Moguls, have passed away before them, yet Islam itself is a thing of indestructible
vitality, and may thrive the more when rid of the magnificent corruptions and the illusory prestige of the
Stamboul successors of the Prophet. In truth, Islam
has existed for centuries in spite of Osmanlee rule, and
not because of it; and this the embassadors lately sent
to the Porte from the most distant parts of the Mussulman world—from Bokhara and Khotan, from the
Sultan of Atchin and the Sultan of the Panthays—
must have learned to their cost, when they found that
the so-called Commander of the Faithful was sufficiently employed nearer home, and had neither the power
nor the will to give them the help or even the advice
they asked.

Mohammedanism, therefore, can still renew its youth,
and it is possible that the present generation, in face of
the advance of semi-barbarous and intolerant Russia,
may see a revival of the old crusading spirit—an outburst of stern fanaticism, which, armed with the courage of despair, obliterating, as in the Circassian war,*

---

* See Baron Von Haxthausen's " Tribes of the Caucasus ;" especially
his interesting account of the rise of Muridism, and the heroic struggle of
Schamyl, his personal influence, and his genius for military and political
organization. Truly while Mohammedanism can throw off geniuses like
Schamyl, it may well be able to dispense with such governments as that

even the immemorial schism of Sonnee and Sheeah, may hurl once more the united strength of the Crescent upon the vanguard of advancing Christendom. It is a prospect formidable to every Christian Power—formidable above all to those who for good or for evil rule thirty millions of Mussulmans in India; but I can not think, even if the result were to be that a stop should be put to all further conquests of Europeans in the East, that the world would be altogether a loser thereby. In the East a revived Islam contains more elements of hope for the future than a corrupt Christianity —and Christianity in Asia has rarely been otherwise than dead ;* and the religious enthusiasm of some new Commander of the Faithful—of some heroic Schamyl or Abdel Kader on a vaster scale—than the dull, heavy tread of military despotism beneath the shadow of the Czars of all the Russias.

---

of the Turks. The Baron's prophecies of a general collapse of Mohammedanism are being signally falsified. The union of Sonnees and Sheeahs was one principle of Muridism as taught by Moollah Mohammed, and after him by Schamyl.

\* For the marked superiority, for instance, of the tribes of the Caucasus which are Mohammedan, to those which are nominally Christian, see Freshfield's "Caucasus," p. 454–457 : " In the Caucasus the traveler will be compelled to contrast the truthfulness, industry, and courteous hospitality of the Mohammedans north of the chain with the lying indolence and churlishness of the Christians in the south ;" and for the general subject of Oriental Christianity as it is found in Armenia, Georgia, Syria, Egypt, etc., see Palgrave's essay entitled " Eastern Christians."

And here, perhaps, will be the place to make a few remarks upon a subject which can not have failed to attract the attention of the more thoughtful among us in recent years—I mean the attempt made to introduce Western manners and customs into Eastern countries.

We live in days when we hear of Khans and Khedives, Shahs and Sultans, giving up their immemorial passivity and seclusion, and even coming to Europe with the avowed intention of carrying back to Asia what they can of Western science and civilization. I should be slow, indeed, to complain of any steps taken by the Western Powers to do away with any institutions which, like the Suttee, the festivals of Juggernaut, the East African slave-trade, or the traffic in opium, are a curse to our common humanity, or are not grounded on any fundamental peculiarity of the Eastern world. But to attempt by force, or even by influence brought to bear upon Eastern rulers, to do away with any domestic or national institutions, such as the form of government or patriarchal slavery, or even polygamy, can do no good.

Eastern despotism is not what Western despotism is, nor is Oriental slavery like American. Nor is even polygamy in the East so intolerable an evil as it would be in the social freedom of the West. For example, an Eastern sovereign has all the power over his subjects that a father had in the most primitive times, and had even in Rome, over his children. His power is liable to the same abuses; but it has also some of its safe-guards and redeeming points. To introduce into his government, as the Shah has been supposed to wish, a system of Boards and Parliaments, of checks and counter-checks, such as works fairly well in this coun-try, because it has grown with our growth and is suit-able to our instinct of compromise in every thing, would be to make many tyrants instead of one, and to cripple the power and lessen the responsibility of the only man in Persia whose interest it is to let no one commit injustice but himself. Asia, till its whole nat-ure be changed, can probably never be better governed than it was by the early Kaliphs; and if an Abou Bakr or an Omar, or even a Haroun or a Mahmoud, a Baber or an Akbar, do not come twice in a century, it is prob-able that Nature has endowed Asiatics with precisely those qualities of patience, docility, and inertness which harmonize better with the evils of such a government than with those of any other.

Polygamy is a more difficult question, and it is im-possible, for obvious reasons, to discuss it adequately here. It is a gigantic evil, worse even than slavery; for with its attendant mischiefs, so far as it extends, it does away with all real sympathy and companionship

between man and woman; it is unnatural in the fullest
sense of the word, in a highly civilized nation, for Nature, by making the number of men and women equal,
has declared decisively for monogamy. But, in a barbarous people, polygamy has this one redeeming point,
that it is less likely that any woman will be left without
a natural protector; and, as a matter of fact, it is almost universally allowed in primitive stages of civilization.* In the East it is the almost inevitable result of
that fundamental institution of Eastern as well as of
Moslem society, the absolute seclusion of women. There
is an impervious bar to all social intercourse between
the sexes before marriage. The husband's knowledge
of his future wife is at second hand only, and rests on
the report of a Khatibeh,† or professional match-maker.
Such a marriage is more than a lottery; there can be
no affection to begin with, and, except on rare occasions,

---

* In an uncivilized nation, split up, as Arabia was before Mohammed,
into a number of hostile tribes, or overrun by its more powerful neighbors, as was Palestine in the time of the Judges, the number of births
of men and women is no doubt about equal; but the male population is
reduced by war to half its proper number; the preponderance of women
in such a state of society renders polygamy possible, and the insecurity renders it from that one point of view allowable. Sir Samuel Baker, in his
"Albert Nyanza," Introduction, p. 25, remarks that "in all tropical countries polygamy is the prevailing evil." He might have gone on to say much
the same of slavery; but then what would become of the charge he so oft-
en makes against Islam—that it is responsible for polygamy and slavery?

† Lane's "Modern Egyptians," vol. i., p. 199.

it is not likely that it will turn out to be really happy. If it be thoroughly uncongenial, a man tries his luck once more in the same miserable lottery, and for his own happiness, and probably also for that of all concerned, annuls the previous bond. Hence polygamy implies freedom of divorce, and both together are the inevitable result of the seclusion of the female sex. But to abolish by law the two former, without dealing with the far more fundamental institution which is its root, would be to carry on a war with symptoms only, and to introduce evils worse than those it is wished to prevent. The only way of going to the root of the matter would be, if it were possible, to allow a freer intercourse between the sexes at all times; Sir William Muir allows that this could not be done at all with the present freedom of divorce.* It is a melancholy fact, but a fact still, that the strict checks imposed by Mohammed on married women, degrading though they are,† are essential to prevent what is still worse, and, be it remembered, what was far worse before the reforms and limitations which Mohammed himself imposed. It is a complete dead-lock; and the greatest reformers, Moses no less than Mohammed, have been unable to deal with the root of the evil. It is to be

---

* Muir, vol. iii., p. 234, and note.
† Sura xxxiii., 6, 56. Also Sura xxiv., 32.

remembered, on the other hand, that both Moses and Mohammed did what they could to restrain and modify its abuses; and at present neither polygamy nor divorce is so common as is often supposed. The humanity of human nature has asserted itself; and Lane, the most accurate observer, says that polygamy is in Egypt at all events very rare among the higher classes, and not common among the lower.*

Much the same may be said of slavery. The slavery of the East is a patriarchal institution, coeval with the very dawn of history. It is an institution allowed and modified by Moses, even as it was allowed and modified by Mohammed, for people in that stage of civilization which required it. In neither nation has it any thing in common with slavery as it was in America, or slavery as practiced at all by civilized nations. To do away with it by force, as has been the case in Khiva, though we naturally rejoice at it, will probably do little permanent good. It will revive in another, and probably a worse shape. Perhaps we have hit upon the one pos-

---

* Lane, vol. i., p. 231: "Not more than one husband in twenty has two wives at the same time." But divorce is very common. If it were not for Lane's proverbial accuracy, one would be inclined to suspect that in the passage referred to in the text he had transposed the words higher and lower. Certainly in other parts of the Mohammedan world polygamy is, for obvious reasons, much more common among the rich than among the poor. But the current of opinion, like the general conditions of society, seems to be every where setting against it, especially in India.

sible means of gradually getting rid of it, in making it impossible to recruit slavery from without by means of the slave-trade. Much will have to be done hencefor-ward by free labor in Arabia, in Persia, and in Egypt, which has hitherto been done by slaves; and we need not fear but that the result will be so good that even in a stolid Oriental people the gradual movement will be one in the direction of abolition. The foreign slave-trade, in fact, is, owing to the remonstrances of Dr. Livingstone and the expeditions of Sir Samuel Baker and Sir Bartle Frere, already, for the time at all events, almost at an end, and it is a mistake to suppose that it ever received any sanction either from Moses or Mo-hammed. Moses ordered the man-stealer and the man-seller to be put to death.* Mohammed is reported by the "Sonnah" to have said, "The worst of men is the seller of man."†

Western science, with its railways, its canals, and its printing-presses, may, no doubt, do something for the material prosperity of Eastern countries, but by itself it

---

* Exodus xxi., 16.

† The slave-trade rests for its support on no religion at all, but only on that which is cruel and selfish in human nature. It is no more fair to tax Islam, as is often done, with the horrors of the East African slave-trade, than it would have been in the last century to tax Christianity with the still greater horrors of the West African traffic and its *sequelæ* in America. It has been remarked with truth that the cruel treatment of domesticated slaves is the shameful and exclusive prerogative of civilization.

will do little for their moral welfare; and a thin varnish of Western civilization, introduced by rulers who have been forced to admire the material power of the West, and have lost their own self-respect in the process, is earnestly to be deprecated. Those Orientals who have been most influenced by the Franco-mania of Stamboul are, beyond all comparison, the most degraded and profligate of their race, and no earnest observer can wish to see imported into other parts of the Mohammedan world that indescribable combination of all that is contemptible in human nature conveyed by the word Levantine.

The heroic and unselfish lives of a few such men as Livingstone—alas that it is now all too certain that his life is a thing of the past!—are the only legitimate means of introducing into semi-civilized countries such benefits as we think we have to bestow. A life and character like Livingstone's has done more to regenerate the African races than any amount of direct preaching, or any number of European settlements, with the miserable and immoral wars that so often follow in their train. Such men are the true pioneers of civilization and Christianity—of the only species of civilization and the only form of Christianity which we have any reason to expect will be a real benefit to the East.

But does it follow, from what I have said of the immobility of the East, that it is impossible for Islam to make any advance at all; that it is impossible for it to yield any thing to the progressive civilization of Christianity and of the West?

How Christianity and civilization should deal with Mohammedanism I have partly indicated already, and shall have a very few more words to say upon the subject presently. But, first, what can Islam do on its part? Where religion and law are indissolubly bound up together, as they are in the Koran, each loses and each gains something. What they gain in stability, they more than lose in flexibility. And yet it may be safely said that there is nothing more extraordinary in the whole history of Islam than the way in which the theory of the verbal inspiration of the Koran, and the consequent stereotyped and unalterable nature of its precepts, have, by ingenuity, by legal fictions, by the "Sonnah," or traditional sayings of Mohammed, and by *responsa prudentum,* been accommodated to the changing circumstances and the various degrees of civilization of the nations which profess it. When the Kadi fails to find in the law laid down for the nomad Arabs a rule precisely applicable to the more complex requirements of Smyrna or of Delhi, he places the sacred volume upon his head, and so renders homage to human reason and to the law of progress. He does what Puritans and Churchmen would alike do well to remember, when each professes to find in the varying or convertible expressions of the writers of the New Testament a divinely ordered and unalterable model of Church government.*  It is not, therefore, quite so true as is commonly supposed that Islam is reconcilable with one narrow form of government or society only; and it is quite possible that where so much has been done already, more may be done in future, and means may be found for reconciling, for instance, the laws against taking interest for money with the requirements of modern society.  The intolerant principles of the Koran have long since been reconciled, except where there is a passing outburst of fanaticism, with the utmost practical toleration; and the standard of the "Jihad," or holy war, will probably never henceforward be raised on an extensive scale except in a war of self-defense, and unless the lives and liberties of Mohammedans, as well as their religion, are at stake.

And, what is infinitely more important, it seems to me that while Mohammedans cling as strongly as ever to their rigid Monotheism, and to their unfaltering be-

---

* Compare Acts xx., 17, μετεκαλέσατο τοὺς πρεσβυτέρους τῆς ἐκκλησίας, with ver. 28, ὑμᾶς . . . ἔθετο ἐπισκόπους. The watchwords of the bitterest ecclesiastical jealousy and hatred are in this passage of the New Testament seen to be, after all, synonymous and convertible terms.

lief in the divine mission of their Prophet—and what serious person could wish them to do otherwise—to give up those beliefs which have made them what they are, which have given them a glorious history, and which have influenced half a world; to give up—

> ". . . Those first affections,
>   Those shadowy recollections,
>  Which, be they what they may,
>  Are yet the fountain-light of all their day,
>   Are yet a master-light of all their seeing;
>    Uphold them—cherish—and have power to make
>  Their noisy years seem moments in the being
>   Of the eternal silence: truths that wake
>      To perish never!"

while they cling, I say, to these as strongly, yes, more strongly than ever, they may yet be brought to see that there is a distinction between what Mohammed said himself and what others have said for him; and that there is a still broader distinction between what he said as a legislator and as a conqueror, and what he said as a simple prophet. There are some among them who see now, and there will be more who will soon see, that there may be an appeal to the Mohammed of Mecca from the Mohammed of Medina; that there may be an idolatry of a book, as well as of a picture, or a statue, or a shapeless mass of stone; and that the Prophet, who always in other matters asserted his fallibility, was never more fallible, though certainly never more sincere, than when he claimed an equal infallibility for the whole Koran alike. Finally, with the growth of knowledge of the real character of our faith, Mohammedans must recognize that the Christ of the Gospel was something ineffably. above the Christ of those Christians from whom alone Mohammed drew his notions of him; that he was a perfect mirror of that one primary attribute of the Eternal of which Mohammed could catch only a far-off glance, and which, had it been shown to him as it really was, must needs have taken possession of his soul.

All this may or may not be in our own time; but in a sympathetic study even of Mohammedanism as it is, Christians have not a little to gain. There is the protest against Polytheism in all its shapes; there is the absolute equality of man before God; there is the sense of the dignity of human nature; there is the simplicity of life, the vivid belief in God's providence, the entire submission to his will; and last, not least, there is the courage of their convictions, the fearless avowal before men of their belief in God, and their pride in its possession as the one thing needful. There is in the lives of average Mohammedans, from whatever causes, less of self-indulgence, less of the mad race for wealth, less of servility, than is to be found in the lives of average Christians. Truly we may think that these things ought not so to be; and if Christians generally were as ready to confess

Christ, and to be proud of being his servants, as Mohammedans are of being followers of Mohammed, one chief obstacle to the spread of Christianity would be removed. And the two great religions which started from kindred soil, the one from Mecca, the other from Jerusalem, might work on in their respective spheres—the one the religion of progress, the other of stability; the one of a complex life, the other of a simple life; the one dwelling more upon the inherent weakness of human nature, the other on its inherent dignity;* the one the religion of the best parts of Asia and Africa, the other of Europe and America—each rejoicing in the success of the other, each supplying the other's wants in a generous rivalry for the common good of humanity.

A few words more about Mohammed himself, and I have done. The world, in its wisdom or unwisdom, has never thought proper to distinguish Mohammed from the millions of Mohammeds named after him by calling him "the Great." Perhaps he was too great for such an external distinction. People call the conqueror of Constantinople, eight centuries later, Mohammed the Second. But I do not think they ever speak of the Prophet as Mohammed the First; and perhaps the unconscious homage thus rendered to him by a world which

---

* Perhaps the two views are, after all, only different aspects of the same truth.

ostensibly, and till very lately, has done him such scant justice, is the highest tribute that can be given to his greatness. The Greeks paid the highest compliment they could to the surpassing splendor of the King of Persia when, consciously or unconsciously, they dropped the article before his name, and so put him on a level, grammatical and moral, with the sun, the moon, and the earth, which could by no possibility need any such distinguishing mark. Compare Mohammed with the long roll of men whom the world by common consent has called " Great;" while I admit that there is no one point in his character in which he is not surpassed by one or other, take him all in all, what he was, and what he did, and what those inspired by him have done, he seems to me to stand alone, above and beyond them all. A distinguished writer on the Holy Roman Empire has remarked of Charles the Great that, " like all the foremost men of our race, he was all great things in one."* But though Mr. Bryce does not illustrate the truth of his remark by Mohammed—nay, by not including him among the foremost men of the world whom he goes on to enumerate, he seems designedly to exclude him—I venture to think that of no one of them all is this remark more strictly true.

---

* Bryce's " Holy Roman Empire," p. 73.

Mohammed did not, indeed, himself conquer a world like Alexander or Cæsar or Napoleon. He did not himself weld together into a homogeneous whole a vast system of states like Charles the Great. He was not a philosophic king like Marcus Aurelius; nor a philosopher like Aristotle or like Bacon, ruling by pure reason the world of thought for centuries with a more than kingly power; he was not a legislator for all mankind, nor even the highest part of it, like Justinian; nor did he cheaply earn the title of " the Great " by being the first among rulers to turn, like Constantine, from the setting to the rising sun. He was not a universal philanthropist, like the greatest of the Stoics—

"Non sibi sed toti genitum se credere mundo;"

nor was he the apostle of the highest form of religion and civilization combined, like Gregory or Boniface, like Leo or Alfred the Great. He was less, indeed, than most of these in one or two of the elements that go to make up human greatness, but he was also greater. Half Christian and half Pagan, half civilized and half barbarian, it was given to him in a marvelous degree to unite the peculiar excellences of the one with the peculiar excellences of the other. " I have seen," said the embassador sent by the triumphant Koreishites to the despised exile at Medina—" I have seen the Persian Chosroes and the Greek Heraclius sitting upon their thrones, but never did I see a man ruling his equals as does Mohammed."

Head of the State as well as of the Church, he was Cæsar and Pope in one; but he was Pope without the Pope's pretensions, and Cæsar without the legions of Cæsar. Without a standing army, without a body-guard, without a palace, without a fixed revenue, if ever any man had the right to say that he ruled by a right divine, it was Mohammed; for he had all the power without its instruments and without its supports. He rose superior to the titles and ceremonies, the solemn trifling and the proud humility of court etiquette. To hereditary kings, to princes born in the purple, these things are, naturally enough, as the breath of life; but those who ought to have known better, even self-made rulers, and those the foremost in the files of time — a Cæsar, a Cromwell, a Napoleon — have been unable to resist their tinsel attractions. Mohammed was content with the reality, he cared not for the dressings, of power.* The simplicity of his private life was in keeping with his public life. "God," says Al Bokhari, "offered him the keys of the treasures of the earth, but he would not accept them."

Hagiology is not history; but the contemporaries of

---

* See "British Quarterly Review," Jan., 1872, p. 128.

Mohammed, his enemies who rejected his mission, with one voice extol his piety, his justice, his veracity, his clemency, his humility, and that at a time before any imaginary sanctity could have enveloped him. A Christian even, as is remarked by a great writer whom I have quoted above, with his more perfect code of morality before him, must admit that Mohammed, with very rare exceptions, practiced all the moral virtues but one; and in that one, as I have shown, he was in advance of his time and nation.

Assuredly, if Christian missionaries are ever to win over Mohammedans to Christianity, they must alter their tactics. It will not be by discrediting the great Arabian Prophet, nor by throwing doubts upon his mission, but by paying him that homage which is his due ; by pointing out, not how Mohammedanism differs from Christianity, but how it resembles it ; by dwelling less on the dogmas of Christianity, and more on its morality ; by showing how perfectly that Christ whom Mohammed with his half-knowledge so reverenced came up to the ideal which prophets and kings desired to see, and had not seen, and which Mohammed himself, Prophet and King in one, could only half realize. In this way, and in this alone, is it likely that Christianity can ever act upon Mohammedanism; not by sweeping it into oblivion—for what of truth there is in it, and there is very much truth, can never die — but by gradually, and perhaps unconsciously, breathing into its vast and still vigorous frame a newer, a purer, and a diviner life.

By a fortune absolutely unique in history, Mohammed is a threefold founder—" of a nation, of an empire, and of a religion." Illiterate himself, scarcely able to read or write, he was yet the author of a book which is a poem, a code of laws, a Book of Common Prayer, and a Bible in one, and is reverenced to this day by a sixth of the whole human race as a miracle of purity of style, of wisdom, and of truth. It was the one miracle claimed by Mohammed — his " standing miracle" he called it; and a miracle indeed it is. But looking at the circumstances of the time, at the unbounded reverence of his followers, and comparing him with the Fathers of the Church or with mediæval saints, to my mind the most miraculous thing about Mohammed is that he never claimed the power of working miracles. Whatever he had said he could do, his disciples would straightway have seen him do. They could not help attributing to him miraculous acts which he never did, and which he always denied he could do. What more crowning proof of his sincerity is needed? Mohammed to the end of his life claimed for himself that title only with which he had begun, and which the highest philosophy and the truest Christianity will one day, I venture to believe, agree in yielding to him—that of a Prophet, a very Prophet of God.

The religion, indeed, that he taught is below the purest form of our own, as the central figure of the Mohammedan religion is below the central figure of the Christian — a difference vast and incommensurable; but, in my opinion, he comes next to him in the long roll of the great benefactors of the human race; next to him, *longo intervallo* certainly, but still next. He had faults, and great ones, which he was always the first himself, according to his light, to confess and to deplore; and the best homage we can render to the noble sincerity of his character is to state them, as I hope I have tried to do, exactly as they were. "It was the fashion of old," to quote once more the words of our greatest novelist and greatest psychologist—and so to conclude this course of Lectures, of the manifold imperfections and shortcomings of which no one of those who have so kindly listened to me week after week can be half so conscious as myself—" It was the fashion of old, when an ox was led out for sacrifice to Jupiter, to chalk the dark spots, and give the offering a false show of unblemished whiteness. Let us fling away the chalk, and boldly say—the victim *is* spotted, but it is not therefore in vain that his mighty heart is laid on the altar of men's highest hopes."

# APPENDICES.

## APPENDIX TO LECTURE I.

SIR BARTLE FRERE, in an interesting and able and catholic essay in "The Church and the Age" on Indian Missions, takes a hopeful view of the future of India as influenced by Western civilization and Christianity. He be
gins (p. 318) by showing, rightly enough, that almost every thing we do in India tends to break up old beliefs, and
so to prepare the way for a new one, and is, therefore, more
or less missionary work; "not only railways and printing-
presses, education, commerce, and the electric telegraph;
our impartial codes and uniform system of administration;
but our misfortunes and our mistakes, our wars, our fam-
ines, and our mutinies." He then gives (p. 334–337) elaborate statistics of the missionary agencies at work in 1865 in
Western India; they have enormously increased in the last
thirty years, and he estimates the number of missionaries
at work at about 105, and the number of converts at somewhere about 2200; and this, multiplied by six or seven,
would probably, he thinks, give a general idea of the direct results of missionary work during that period through-

out all India (I would remark here that an official statement published in 1873 gives a much more favorable account, estimating the number of communicants at 78,494);
but when Sir Bartle Frere comes to deal with Mohammedanism (p. 354–356), he gives no statistics on the point we
most desiderate—the number of converts, if it be at all
appreciable, from Islam to Christianity; the general remarks, indeed, he does make, seem to me to go exactly
contrary to the conclusions he draws from them—*e. g.*,
Mohammedans study portions of the Bible more than they
did formerly; but these portions unfortunately seem to be
the prophetical writings, especially those of Daniel; and
they find therein the denunciations of Christianity which
Christians find in it against other creeds; they are humil-
iated by the fact that Mohammedanism is no longer the
imperial creed of India; but the upshot of their depression
is not Christianity, but Wahhabeeism, *i. e.*, a return to Islam
in its simplest and sternest shape. Brahmoism, which is
really Brahmanism as modified by Christianity—Brahmanism *minus* caste and *minus* idolatry of every kind—seems
to be in some respects the beginning of a national movement, and, judging from the authoritative sermon (p. 346–
352) delivered in Calcutta on the thirty-ninth anniversary
of the Brahma Samaj, and entitled "The Future Church,"
seems to me to give real hope for the future, and to be
very suggestive as to the way in which missionaries should
go to work. "The answer," says the preacher, "of Jesus
the immortal Son of God, Thou shalt love the Lord thy

God with all thy heart, and with all thy mind, and with all thy soul, and with all thy strength, and thy neighbor as thyself, is the essence of true religion simply and exhaustively expounded." "The composite faith of the future Church is to combine in perfect harmony the profound devotion of the Hindoo and the heroic enthusiasm of the Mussulman;" but, unfortunately, the simplicity and intelligibility of the Mohammedan creed render it incapable at present of actually coalescing with the eclectic spirit of Brahmoism. It is strange at first sight that Mohammedanism, originally the most eclectic of religions, should, in India at all events, prove itself to be the least capable of settling down on terms of equality with other creeds, or of combining with them. No doubt the fact that Mohammedanism has been the imperial creed and is so no longer, and the proud memories of Mahmoud and Akbar, of Baber and of Aurungzebe, are a formidable, though it is to be hoped a passing, difficulty. If the Mohammedan revival now going on in India under the influence of the Wahhabees, the Firazees, and the followers of Dudu Miyan, can only be accompanied by a great moral reformation, such as Sprenger himself does not seem to despair of (vol. i., p. 459—"the Arabs only want another Luther"), the result, partially at least, of Christian influences, the simplicity of Islam will no doubt in its turn give it a great advantage over the Brahma Samaj in the struggle to fill the void created by the crumbling fabric of Hindooism. It has another great advantage in being already to some extent in

possession of the ground.   I observe that one of the speak-
ers at the recent Allahabad Missionary Conference says
that thirty millions, the estimated number of Mussulmans
in India, is much below the mark.

The unfavorable opinion expressed by Dr. Livingstone
on the effects of Mohammedanism in Africa ("Expedition
to the Zambesi," p. 513–516, and 602–603) appears opposed
to the general view I have taken in the Lecture; and of
course, so far as his personal experience goes, is unim-
peachable and conclusive.   But it is clear that Dr. Livingstone drew his general conclusions almost entirely from
his acquaintance with the Arab slave-traders in the south
and east of Africa, whom it was the main purpose of his
noble and heroic life to put down.   In the Lecture I have
purposely not dwelt upon the extension of Islam along the
coast to the south of the Equator, for the simple reason
that the inhabitants are Mohammedans in nothing but the
name.   The Arabs there are of the most degraded type,
and are engaged almost to a man in the brutalizing slave-
trade, which by itself is a complete obstacle to every species of civilization and religion.   No doubt, as Dr. Livingstone remarks, the native African there contrasts favorably
with the Mohammedan—as favorably, I would add, as he
does even with the Portuguese; but that Dr. Livingstone
judged of the whole of Mohammedan Africa by his experience of its worst part is clear from his remark—opposed
as it is to the unanimous testimony of travelers in Northern and Central Africa—" that the only foundation for the

statements respecting the spread of Islam in Africa is the fact that in a remote corner of Northwest Africa the Foulahs and Mandingoes, and some other tribes in Northern Africa, have made conquests of territory; but that even they care so little for the extension of their faith, that after conquest no pains whatever are taken to indoctrinate the adults of the tribe" (p. 513). Captain Burton asserts that "Mohammedans alone make proselytes in Africa." Dr. Livingstone says as explicitly "in Africa the followers of Christ alone are anxious to propagate their faith." Here is a direct contradiction; and it is obvious that in a country of such vast extent as Africa no such sweeping statement can be absolutely true. Perhaps Sierra Leone, to which Dr. Livingstone paid a visit for the purpose of testing the results of missionary enterprise, and to which he specially refers (p. 663), will furnish us with the best materials for pointing out how far the two statements are reconcilable with each other, and with substantial accuracy. In Sierra Leone there is a large negro community, the members of which having been brought for many years into contact not only with direct Christian preaching, but, what is more important, with Christian education, government, and example, are both excellent citizens and sincere Christians, and, as one would expect, contrast favorably in point of morality even with the best Mohammedans. This is unquestionably true; and of the self-denying efforts of the missionaries, especially the native ones, within certain limits, it is impossible to speak too highly.

As to the exact number of Christians in the colony at this moment it is rather difficult to arrive at an accurate conclusion; but, to take Dr. Livingstone's figures, he remarks (p. 605) that in the census of 1861 the whole population of Sierra Leone itself was 41,000 souls, 27,000 of them being Christian, and 1774 Mohammedan—"not a very large proportion," he observes, "for the only sect in Africa which makes proselytes." It is not a large proportion, but what is the number now? Sierra Leone now affords the most striking proof that can be given of the extent to which on the one hand Islam is spreading in that part of Africa by the efforts of unassisted missionaries, and on the other of the absence of any such propagation of the Christian faith among the tribes beyond the limits of the settlement. When Dr. Livingstone visited Sierra Leone a few years ago, Islam was, as he says, hardly known there; since then Mohammedan missionaries have come thither from the Foulahs and from the far interior, and with what result? No one will say that it is the sword to which they owe their success, for the peace of Sierra Leone has been for years undisturbed. And now we have (Government Report of West African Colonies, 1873) the testimony of Mr. Johnson (p. 15), the able and excellent missionary whom I have quoted in my Lecture, indorsed as it would seem by the bishop of the diocese, that the Christian community at Sierra Leone, however flourishing itself, has exercised no influence on the large number of native Africans resorting annually to the town for the purpose of trade, and still less has it done any thing to propagate itself by sending out missionaries among adjoining tribes. On the other hand, a few active and zealous Mohammedan missionaries have carried their peaceful war into the enemy's country, and have produced great results even among the Christian and native population of Sierra Leone itself; insomuch that the religion of a large portion, the Governor says of the majority, of the Christians within the settlement has been actually changed by their preaching. There may be, and it is to be hoped there is, exaggeration as to the numbers; but there can be no doubt, looking to the *consensus* of testimony, that Islam is propagated in Western, Northern, and Central Africa; that it is propagated by simple preaching and with marked success, even where a Christian government, and, what is better, Christianity itself, is to a great extent in possession of the ground. One wishes that Dr. Livingstone, the greatest and most single-minded of all the friends of Africa, had himself come into contact with a few of these simple and single-minded Mohammedan missionaries. They come so near in many respects to his own ideal of what a Christian missionary ought to be, that one feels sure he would have been led to modify his judgment as to the system which produces them, and to the great teacher whom he rarely mentions but as the "false prophet."

The remarks I have made in the Lecture as to the attitude which it seems to me that Christian missionaries should adopt, wherever their efforts appear to have a

chance of being successful—and surely there is too much
evil in the world that is remediable to allow of a great
expenditure of labor or money where there is no such
prospect—have been suggested to me mainly by way of
contrast to what I have read in most books devoted to
the cause of Missions.  Even so noble and self-sacrificing
and single-hearted a man as Henry Martyn appears to
have gone out as a missionary to India—nay, to have
argued with Mohammedans—without having first read a
word of the Koran, even in its English dress ("Memoir
of Rev. Henry Martyn," by Rev. J. Sargent, p. 177: cf.
225); and throughout his career he treats it as an "imposture;" "the work of the devil."  He is sent to fight
"the four-faced devil of India"—*i. e.*, Hindoos, Mohammedans, Papists, and Infidels (p. 259); and see a summary
of his written arguments against Mohammedans (on p.
335), which are quite enough by themselves to account
for his ill success.  See also the account by another devoted missionary, the Rev. C. B. Leupolt, of his mission at
Benares ("Recollections of an Indian Missionary"), who
takes much the same position.  "The so-called Prophet
of the Mohammedans;" "the Koran is an assemblage of
facts and passages taken from the Bible, mixed with a
great number of gross and cunningly devised fables;"
"no Mohammedan who believes the whole Koran can
have the notion of the true God;" "the Koran is calcu-
lated to lead man daily farther from God, and to unite
him closer to the Prince of darkness;" "Satan holds them

enthralled by a false religion," and so on. How not to deal with a different faith could hardly be better demonstrated than by the writings of two such admirable and devoted men. Surely the system has been to blame! Happily, as is shown from the general tone of the Allahabad Conference, and the explicit testimony of the Government of India in 1873, there has been a great advance in the right direction lately. Not to go beyond the limited circle of one's own acquaintance, such men as Bishop Cotton; the Rev. George and the Rev. Arthur Moule, now in China; and the Rev. James Johnson, native of Sierra Leone — though I would not venture to say that they would in any degree accept my point of view — yet in reality would have much in common with it; and all would certainly admit the immense amount of good that is to be found in the creeds which it is their duty to controvert. Alas, that those who knew Bishop Cotton well, and who therefore know what his catholic spirit might have done for India, can only now, when they think of him, repeat to themselves, consciously or unconsciously, the touching lament—

> "But oh for a touch of the vanished hand,
> And a sound of the voice that is still!"

# APPENDIX TO LECTURE III.

THAT the assertions I have made in the third Lecture, as to the comparative ferocity of Christian and Mussulman religious wars, are within the mark, it would be easy to bring abundance of proof. I will adduce here one illustration only, drawn from the chief battle-ground of the contending forces, the Holy Land. Jerusalem capitulated to Omar, the third Kaliph, after a protracted blockade, in the year 637. No property was destroyed except in the inevitable operations of the siege, and not a drop of blood was shed except on the field of battle. Omar entered the city with the Patriarch, conversing amicably about its history; at the hour of prayer he was invited by the Patriarch to worship in the Church of the Holy Sepulchre, but he refused to do so for fear that his descendants might claim a similar right, and so the freedom of religious worship, which he wished to secure to the inhabitants by the articles of capitulation, might be endangered. In the year 1099 the Holy City fell before the arms of the Crusaders after a much shorter siege. It was taken by storm, and for three days there was an indiscriminate slaughter of men, women, and children; 70,000 Mussulmans were put to the sword, 10,000 of them in the mosque of Omar itself: "*in eodem templo decem millia de-*

*collata sunt; pedites nostri usque ad bases cruore peremptorum tingebantur, nec feminis nec parvulis pepercerunt.*"
This comes not from an enemy, but from the monkish historian, an eye-witness and a partaker of what he relates, Foulcher of Chartres. Raymond of Argiles and Daimbert, Archbishop of Pisa, give similar details, and all with approval. The city itself was pillaged; but the turn of the Saracens came once more in the year 1187. The breach was already forced, when the great Saladin retracted a hasty vow he had made to avenge the innocent blood that had been shed when the city had been sacked by the Crusaders, and took not Godfrey de Bouillon but Omar for his model. No blood was shed, and the captives were allowed to ransom themselves, the Frankish Christians leaving the city, the Eastern Christians continuing in peace.

As to humanity in war in general, the progress made has not been so great as is commonly supposed, even among those who pride themselves—and who to some extent pride themselves with reason—on being the pioneers of Christianity and civilization. Take the case of Africa. I am not aware that the Saracens in the full career of conquest deliberately burned a single city in the whole of the North of Africa, whether as a precautionary measure, or to support their prestige, or to glut their revenge. Can England say the same? If we assume—a large assumption—that the war on the Gold Coast in 1874 is wholly justifiable, if we also assume that the burning of the enemy's capital was indeed a necessity, it was a necessity for which a Christian nation should go into mourning, and should contemplate not with feelings of triumph, but with those of humiliation and regret. Is there any thing of the kind, or has one single ruler either in Church or State—now that the elections are over, and the moral iniquity of the war has been condoned by its success—been heard to raise his voice in condemnation of it, as even Omar or Saladin might have done? It is difficult to see how the English nation, which has abolished the slave-trade in the West of Africa, and is in its best portions profoundly philanthropic, can honestly believe that they are advancing the objects they have at heart when, in support of such a treaty as I have alluded to in the Lecture, they lead on a weaker barbarous nation, whom *pro hac vice* we designate as "our allies," against a more powerful one, and deliberately burn out of their homes a people who, barbarous and cruel as they were, have offended us not by their cruelty or by their human sacrifices, but by their honest belief that we had come to Africa to bar them from access to their own coast. It seems not to have occurred to any one that our "prestige" would have been sufficiently vindicated, and our future security sufficiently provided for, if we had burned down the palace of the king, the chief offender. But our "prestige" serves as an ample excuse for committing what we should condemn as crimes in any other nation. It is an entity that has juggled us into the belief that to destroy what we can not retain and can not use is the prerogative, not of barbarism, but of civilization and of Christianity. Had the war upon the Gold Coast been avowedly a war not for the spread of our influence, or for the security of a territory acquired by questionable means, but a moral crusade against human sacrifice, or for any purely unselfish object, the case would have been different. Truly this war will be a *damnosa hereditas* to posterity, alike whether we accept or disclaim the fearful responsibilities in which it has involved us.

There is an anecdote related of Mahmoud the Ghaznevide, the great Turkish conqueror of Central Asia, which seems to me to be suggestive. Soon after the conquest of Persia, a caravan was cut off by robbers in one of its deserts, and the mother of one of the merchants who was killed went to Ghazni to complain. Mahmoud urged the impossibility of keeping order in so remote a part of his territories, when the woman boldly answered: "Why, then, do you take countries which you can not govern, and for the protection of which you must answer in the Day of Judgment?" Mahmoud was struck with the reproach; whether it would have prevented all further conquests on his part we do not know, for he died soon afterward; but he liberally rewarded the woman, and took immediate and effectual steps for the protection of the caravans.

*Babylonian Influence on the Bible and Popular Beliefs: A Comparative Study of Genesis I.2,* by A. Smythe Palmer. ISBN 1-58509-000-X • 124 pages • 6 x 9 • trade paper • $12.95

*Biography of Satan: Exposing the Origins of the Devil,* by Kersey Graves. ISBN 1-885395-11-6 • 168 pages • 5 1/2 x 8 1/2 • trade paper • $13.95

*The Malleus Maleficarum: The Notorious Handbook Once Used to Condemn and Punish "Witches",* by Heinrich Kramer and James Sprenger. ISBN 1-58509-098-0 • 332 pages • 6 x 9 • trade paper • $25.95

*Crux Ansata: An Indictment of the Roman Catholic Church,* by H. G. Wells. ISBN 1-58509-210-X • 160 pages • 6 x 9 • trade paper • $14.95

*Emanuel Swedenborg: The Spiritual Columbus,* by U.S.E. (William Spear). ISBN 1-58509-096-4 • 208 pages • 6 x 9 • trade paper • $17.95

*Dragons and Dragon Lore,* by Ernest Ingersoll. ISBN 1-58509-021-2 • 228 pages • 6 x 9 • trade paper • illustrated • $17.95

*The Vision of God,* by Nicholas of Cusa. ISBN 1-58509-004-2 • 160 pages • 5 x 8 • trade paper • $13.95

*The Historical Jesus and the Mythical Christ: Separating Fact From Fiction,* by Gerald Massey. ISBN 1-58509-073-5 • 244 pages • 6 x 9 • trade paper • $18.95

*Gog and Magog: The Giants in Guildhall; Their Real and Legendary History, with an Account of Other Giants at Home and Abroad,* by F.W. Fairholt. ISBN 1-58509-084-0 • 172 pages • 6 x 9 • trade paper • $16.95

*The Origin and Evolution of Religion,* by Albert Churchward. ISBN 1-58509-078-6 • 504 pages • 6 x 9 • trade paper • $39.95

*The Origin of Biblical Traditions,* by Albert T. Clay. ISBN 1-58509-065-4 • 220 pages • 5 1/2 x 8 1/2 • trade paper • $17.95

*Aryan Sun Myths,* by Sarah Elizabeth Titcomb. Introduction by Charles Morris. ISBN 1-58509-069-7 • 192 pages • 6 x 9 • trade paper • $15.95

*The Social Record of Christianity,* by Joseph McCabe. Includes *The Lies and Fallacies of the Encyclopedia Britannica,* ISBN 1-58509-215-0 • 204 pages • 6 x 9 • trade paper • $17.95

*The History of the Christian Religion and Church During the First Three Centuries,* by Dr. Augustus Neander. ISBN 1-58509-077-8 • 112 pages • 6 x 9 • trade paper • $12.95

*Ancient Symbol Worship: Influence of the Phallic Idea in the Religions of Antiquity,* by Hodder M. Westropp and C. Staniland Wake. ISBN 1-58509-048-4 • 120 pages • 6 x 9 • trade paper • illustrated • $12.95

*The Gnosis: Or Ancient Wisdom in the Christian Scriptures,* by William Kingsland. ISBN 1-58509-047-6 • 232 pages • 6 x 9 • trade paper • $18.95

*The Evolution of the Idea of God: An Inquiry into the Origin of Religions,* by Grant Allen. ISBN 1-58509-074-3 • 160 pages • 6 x 9 • trade paper • $14.95

*Sun Lore of All Ages: A Survey of Solar Mythology, Folklore, Customs, Worship, Festivals, and Superstition,* by William Tyler Olcott. ISBN 1-58509-044-1 • 316 pages • 6 x 9 • trade paper • $24.95

*Nature Worship: An Account of Phallic Faiths and Practices Ancient and Modern,* by the Author of Phallicism with an Introduction by Tedd St. Rain. ISBN 1-58509-049-2 • 112 pages • 6 x 9 • trade paper • illustrated • $12.95

*Life and Religion,* by Max Muller. ISBN 1-885395-10-8 • 237 pages • 5 1/2 x 8 1/2 • trade paper • $14.95

*Jesus: God, Man, or Myth? An Examination of the Evidence,* by Herbert Cutner. ISBN 1-58509-072-7 • 304 pages • 6 x 9 • trade paper • $23.95

*Pagan and Christian Creeds: Their Origin and Meaning,* by Edward Carpenter. ISBN 1-58509-024-7 • 316 pages • 5 1/2 x 8 1/2 • trade paper • $24.95

*The Christ Myth: A Study,* by Elizabeth Evans. ISBN 1-58509-037-9 • 136 pages • 6 x 9 • trade paper • $13.95

*Popery: Foe of the Church and the Republic,* by Joseph F. Van Dyke. ISBN 1-58509-058-1 • 336 pages • 6 x 9 • trade paper • illustrated • $25.95

*Career of Religious Ideas,* by Hudson Tuttle. ISBN 1-58509-066-2 • 172 pages • 5 x 8 • trade paper • $15.95

*Buddhist Suttas: Major Scriptural Writings from Early Buddhism,* by T.W. Rhys Davids. ISBN 1-58509-079-4 • 376 pages • 6 x 9 • trade paper • $27.95

*Early Buddhism,* by T. W. Rhys Davids. Includes *Buddhist Ethics: The Way to Salvation?,* by Paul Tice. ISBN 1-58509-076-X • 112 pages • 6 x 9 • trade paper • $12.95

*The Fountain-Head of Religion: A Comparative Study of the Principal Religions of the World and a Manifestation of their Common Origin from the Vedas,* by Ganga Prasad. ISBN 1-58509-054-9 • 276 pages • 6 x 9 • trade paper • $22.95

*India: What Can It Teach Us?,* by Max Muller. ISBN 1-58509-064-6 • 284 pages • 5 1/2 x 8 1/2 • trade paper • $22.95

*Matrix of Power: How the World has Been Controlled by Powerful People Without Your Knowledge,* by Jordan Maxwell. ISBN 1-58509-120-0 • 104 pages • 6 x 9 • trade paper • $12.95

*Cyberculture Counterconspiracy: A Steamshovel Web Reader, Volume One,* edited by Kenn Thomas. ISBN 1-58509-125-1 • 180 pages • 6 x 9 • trade paper • illustrated • $16.95

*Cyberculture Counterconspiracy: A Steamshovel Web Reader, Volume Two,* edited by Kenn Thomas. ISBN 1-58509-126-X • 132 pages • 6 x 9 • trade paper • illustrated • $13.95

*Oklahoma City Bombing: The Suppressed Truth,* by Jon Rappoport. ISBN 1-885395-22-1 • 112 pages • 5 1/2 x 8 1/2 • trade paper • $12.95

*The Protocols of the Learned Elders of Zion,* by Victor Marsden. ISBN 1-58509-015-8 • 312 pages • 6 x 9 • trade paper • $24.95

*Secret Societies and Subversive Movements,* by Nesta H. Webster. ISBN 1-58509-092-1 • 432 pages • 6 x 9 • trade paper • $29.95

*The Secret Doctrine of the Rosicrucians,* by Magus Incognito. ISBN 1-58509-091-3 • 256 pages • 6 x 9 • trade paper • $20.95

*The Origin and Evolution of Freemasonry: Connected with the Origin and Evolution of the Human Race,* by Albert Churchward. ISBN 1-58509-029-8 • 240 pages • 6 x 9 • trade paper • $18.95

*The Lost Key: An Explanation and Application of Masonic Symbols,* by Prentiss Tucker. ISBN 1-58509-050-6 • 192 pages • 6 x 9 • trade paper • illustrated • $15.95

*The Character, Claims, and Practical Workings of Freemasonry,* by Rev. C.G. Finney. ISBN 1-58509-094-8 • 288 pages • 6 x 9 • trade paper • $22.95

*The Secret World Government or "The Hidden Hand": The Unrevealed in History,* by Maj.-Gen., Count Cherep-Spiridovich. ISBN 1-58509-093-X • 270 pages • 6 x 9 • trade paper • $21.95

*The Magus, Book One: A Complete System of Occult Philosophy,* by Francis Barrett. ISBN 1-58509-031-X • 200 pages • 6 x 9 • trade paper • illustrated • $16.95

*The Magus, Book Two: A Complete System of Occult Philosophy,* by Francis Barrett. ISBN 1-58509-032-8 • 220 pages • 6 x 9 • trade paper • illustrated • $17.95

*The Magus, Book One and Two: A Complete System of Occult Philosophy,* by Francis Barrett. ISBN 1-58509-033-6 • 420 pages • 6 x 9 • trade paper • illustrated • $34.90

*The Key of Solomon The King,* by S. Liddell MacGregor Mathers. ISBN 1-58509-022-0 • 152 pages • 6 x 9 • trade paper • illustrated • $12.95

*Magic and Mystery in Tibet,* by Alexandra David-Neel. ISBN 1-58509-097-2 • 352 pages • 6 x 9 • trade paper • $26.95

*The Comte de St. Germain,* by I. Cooper Oakley. ISBN 1-58509-068-9 • 280 pages • 6 x 9 • trade paper • illustrated • $22.95

*Alchemy Rediscovered and Restored,* by A. Cockren. ISBN 1-58509-028-X • 156 pages • 5 1/2 x 8 1/2 • trade paper • $13.95

*The 6th and 7th Books of Moses,* with an Introduction by Paul Tice. ISBN 1-58509-045-X • 188 pages • 6 x 9 • trade paper • illustrated • $16.95

*Of Heaven and Earth: Essays Presented at the First Sitchin Studies Day,* edited by Zecharia Sitchin. ISBN 1-885395-17-5 • 164 pages • 5 1/2 x 8 1/2 • trade paper • illustrated • $14.95

*God Games: What Do You Do Forever?,* by Neil Freer. ISBN 1-885395-39-6 • 312 pages • 6 x 9 • trade paper • $19.95

*Space Travelers and the Genesis of the Human Form: Evidence of Intelligent Contact in the Solar System,* by Joan d'Arc. ISBN 1-58509-127-8 • 208 pages • 6 x 9 • trade paper • illustrated • $18.95

*Humanity's Extraterrestrial Origins: ET Influences on Humankind's Biological and Cultural Evolution,* by Dr. Arthur David Horn with Lynette Mallory-Horn. ISBN 3-931652-31-9 • 373 pages • 6 x 9 • trade paper • $17.00

*Past Shock: The Origin of Religion and Its Impact on the Human Soul,* by Jack Barranger. ISBN 1-885395-08-6 • 126 pages • 6 x 9 • trade paper • illustrated • $12.95

*Flying Serpents and Dragons: The Story of Mankind's Reptilian Past,* by R.A. Boulay. ISBN 1-885395-38-8 • 276 pages • 6 x 9 • trade paper • illustrated • $19.95

*Triumph of the Human Spirit: The Greatest Achievements of the Human Soul and How Its Power Can Change Your Life,* by Paul Tice. ISBN 1-885395-57-4 • 295 pages • 6 x 9 • trade paper • illustrated • $19.95

*Mysteries Explored: The Search for Human Origins, UFOs, and Religious Beginnings,* by Jack Barranger and Paul Tice. ISBN 1-58509-101-4 • 104 pages • 6 x 9 • trade paper • $12.95

*Mushrooms and Mankind: The Impact of Mushrooms on Human Consciousness and Religion,* by James Arthur. ISBN 1-58509-151-0 • 180 pages • 6 x 9 • trade paper • $16.95

*Vril or Vital Magnetism,* with an Introduction by Paul Tice. ISBN 1-58509-030-1 • 124 pages • 5 1/2 x 8 1/2 • trade paper • $12.95

*The Odic Force: Letters on Od and Magnetism,* by Karl von Reichenbach. ISBN 1-58509-001-8 • 192 pages • 6 x 9 • trade paper • $15.95

*The New Revelation: The Coming of a New Spiritual Paradigm,* by Arthur Conan Doyle. ISBN 1-58509-220-7 • 124 pages • 6 x 9 • trade paper • $12.95

*The Astral World: Its Scenes, Dwellers, and Phenomena,* by Swami Panchadasi. ISBN 1-58509-071-9 • 104 pages • 6 x 9 • trade paper • $11.95

*Reason and Belief: The Impact of Scientific Discovery on Religious and Spiritual Faith,* by Sir Oliver Lodge. ISBN 1-58509-226-6 • 180 pages • 6 x 9 • trade paper • $17.95

*William Blake: A Biography,* by Basil De Selincourt. ISBN 1-58509-225-8 • 384 pages • 6 x 9 • trade paper • $28.95

*The Divine Pymander: And Other Writings of Hermes Trismegistus,* translated by John D. Chambers. ISBN 1-58509-046-8 • 196 pages • 6 x 9 • trade paper • $16.95

*Theosophy and The Secret Doctrine,* by Harriet L. Henderson. Includes *H.P. Blavatsky: An Outline of Her Life,* by Herbert Whyte. ISBN 1-58509-075-1 • 132 pages • 6 x 9 • trade paper • $13.95

*The Light of Egypt, Volume One: The Science of the Soul and the Stars,* by Thomas H. Burgoyne. ISBN 1-58509-051-4 • 320 pages • 6 x 9 • trade paper • illustrated • $24.95

*The Light of Egypt, Volume Two: The Science of the Soul and the Stars,* by Thomas H. Burgoyne. ISBN 1-58509-052-2 • 224 pages • 6 x 9 • trade paper • illustrated • $17.95

*The Jumping Frog and 18 Other Stories: 19 Unforgettable Mark Twain Stories,* by Mark Twain. ISBN 1-58509-200-2 • 128 pages • 6 x 9 • trade paper • $12.95

*The Devil's Dictionary: A Guidebook for Cynics,* by Ambrose Bierce. ISBN 1-58509-016-6 • 144 pages • 6 x 9 • trade paper • $12.95

*The Smoky God: Or The Voyage to the Inner World,* by Willis George Emerson. ISBN 1-58509-067-0 • 184 pages • 6 x 9 • trade paper • illustrated • $15.95

*A Short History of the World,* by H.G. Wells. ISBN 1-58509-211-8 • 320 pages • 6 x 9 • trade paper • $24.95

*The Voyages and Discoveries of the Companions of Columbus,* by Washington Irving. ISBN 1-58509-500-1 • 352 pages • 6 x 9 • hard cover • $39.95

*History of Baalbek,* by Michel Alouf. ISBN 1-58509-063-8 • 196 pages • 5 x 8 • trade paper • illustrated • $15.95

*Ancient Egyptian Masonry: The Building Craft,* by Sommers Clarke and R. Engelback. ISBN 1-58509-059-X • 350 pages • 6 x 9 • trade paper • illustrated • $26.95

*That Old Time Religion: The Story of Religious Foundations,* by Jordan Maxwell and Paul Tice. ISBN 1-58509-100-6 • 220 pages • 6 x 9 • trade paper • $19.95

*Jumpin' Jehovah: Exposing the Atrocities of the Old Testament God,* by Paul Tice. ISBN 1-58509-102-2 • 104 pages • 6 x 9 • trade paper • $12.95

*The Book of Enoch: A Work of Visionary Revelation and Prophecy, Revealing Divine Secrets and Fantastic Information about Creation, Salvation, Heaven and Hell,* translated by R. H. Charles. ISBN 1-58509-019-0 • 152 pages • 5 1/2 x 8 1/2 • trade paper • $13.95

*The Book of Enoch: Translated from the Editor's Ethiopic Text and Edited with an Enlarged Introduction, Notes and Indexes, Together with a Reprint of the Greek Fragments,* edited by R. H. Charles. ISBN 1-58509-080-8 • 448 pages • 6 x 9 • trade paper • $34.95

*The Book of the Secrets of Enoch,* translated from the Slavonic by W. R. Morfill. Edited, with Introduction and Notes by R. H. Charles. ISBN 1-58509-020-4 • 148 pages • 5 1/2 x 8 1/2 • trade paper • $13.95

*Enuma Elish: The Seven Tablets of Creation, Volume One,* by L. W. King. ISBN 1-58509-041-7 • 236 pages • 6 x 9 • trade paper • illustrated • $18.95

*Enuma Elish: The Seven Tablets of Creation, Volume Two,* by L. W. King. ISBN 1-58509-042-5 • 260 pages • 6 x 9 • trade paper • illustrated • $19.95

*Enuma Elish, Volumes One and Two: The Seven Tablets of Creation,* by L. W. King. Two volumes from above bound as one. ISBN 1-58509-043-3 • 496 pages • 6 x 9 • trade paper • illustrated • $38.90

*The Archko Volume: Documents that Claim Proof to the Life, Death, and Resurrection of Christ,* by Drs. McIntosh and Twyman. ISBN 1-58509-082-4 • 248 pages • 6 x 9 • trade paper • $20.95

*The Lost Language of Symbolism: An Inquiry into the Origin of Certain Letters, Words, Names, Fairy-Tales, Folklore, and Mythologies,* by Harold Bayley. ISBN 1-58509-070-0 • 384 pages • 6 x 9 • trade paper • $27.95

*The Book of Jasher: A Suppressed Book that was Removed from the Bible, Referred to in Joshua and Second Samuel,* translated by Albinus Alcuin (800 AD). ISBN 1-58509-081-6 • 304 pages • 6 x 9 • trade paper • $24.95

*The Bible's Most Embarrassing Moments,* with an Introduction by Paul Tice. ISBN 1-58509-025-5 • 172 pages • 5 x 8 • trade paper • $14.95

*History of the Cross: The Pagan Origin and Idolatrous Adoption and Worship of the Image,* by Henry Dana Ward. ISBN 1-58509-056-5 • 104 pages • 6 x 9 • trade paper • illustrated • $11.95

*Was Jesus Influenced by Buddhism? A Comparative Study of the Lives and Thoughts of Gautama and Jesus,* by Dwight Goddard. ISBN 1-58509-027-1 • 252 pages • 6 x 9 • trade paper • $19.95

*History of the Christian Religion to the Year Two Hundred,* by Charles B. Waite. ISBN 1-885395-15-9 • 556 pages • 6 x 9 • hard cover • $25.00

*Symbols, Sex, and the Stars,* by Ernest Busenbark. ISBN 1-885395-19-1 • 396 pages • 5 1/2 x 8 1/2 • trade paper • $22.95

*History of the First Council of Nice: A World's Christian Convention, A.D. 325,* by Dean Dudley. ISBN 1-58509-023-9 • 132 pages • 5 1/2 x 8 1/2 • trade paper • $12.95

*The World's Sixteen Crucified Saviors,* by Kersey Graves. ISBN 1-58509-018-2 • 436 pages • 5 1/2 x 8 1/2 • trade paper • $29.95

Printed in the United States
R12290215060301PG7858D007B-8